MYSTICISM IN C. S. LEWIS

Into the Region of Awe

Gene

DAVID C. DOWNING

InterVarsity Press
Downers Grove, Illinois

InterVarsity Press
P.O. Box 1400, Downers Grove, IL 60515-1426
World Wide Web: www.ivpress.com
E-mail: mail@ivpress.com

©2005 by David C. Downing

InterVarsity Press® is the book-publishing division of InterVarsity Christian Fellowship/USA®, a student
movement active on campus at hundreds of universities, colleges and schools of nursing in the United States of
America, and a member movement of the International Fellowship of Evangelical Students. For information
about local and regional activities, write Public Relations Dept., InterVarsity Christian Fellowship/USA, 6400
Schroeder Rd., P.O. Box 7895, Madison, WI 53707-7895, or visit the IVCF website at <www.intervarsity.org>.

All Scripture quotations, unless otherwise indicated, are taken from the Holy Bible, New International
Version®. NIV®. Copyright ©1973, 1978, 1984 by International Bible Society. Used by permission
of Zondervan Publishing House. All rights reserved.

Material from chapter two on the life of C. S. Lewis is adapted from The Most Reluctant Convert: C. S.
Lewis's Journey to Faith by David C. Downing. Copyright 2002 by David C. Downing. Used with permission
of InterVarsity Press, P.O. Box 1400, Downers Grove, IL 60515-1426, <www.ivpress.com>.

Material on Ransom's spiritual journey in the Space Trilogy is adapted from Planets in Peril: A Critical Study
of C. S. Lewis's Ransom Trilogy. Copyright 1992 by David C. Downing. Used by permission of the University
of Massachusetts Press.

Design: Cindy Kiple

Images: clouds: Ruth Sorenson/Illustration Works
          C. S. Lewis photo: Arthur Strong

ISBN 0-8308-3284-X

Printed in the United States of America ∞

Library of Congress Cataloging-in-Publication Data

Downing, David C.
 Into the region of awe: mysticism in C. S. Lewis / by David C.
 Downing.
    p. cm.
 Includes bibliographical references and indexes.
 ISBN 0-8308-3284-X (alk. paper)
 1. Mysticism. 2. Lewis, C. S. (Clive Staples), 1898-1963. I.
 Title.
 BV5082.3.D69 2005
 248.2'2'092—dc22

                                                                                         2004029844

P	18	17	16	15	14	13	12	11	10	9	8	7	6	5	4	3	2	1
Y	18	17	16	15	14	13	12	11	10	09	08	07	06	05				

For Crystal

who blends the love of wisdom

with the wisdom of love

CONTENTS

ACKNOWLEDGMENTS

I would like to thank first two friends of C. S. Lewis whom I am honored to count among my own friends. I am grateful to Walter Hooper for providing me with the context for Lewis's correspondence with Evelyn Underhill and for his thoughtful comments to me about the difference between belief and "suspending disbelief." I am indebted as well to Barbara Reynolds for first calling to my attention some of the parallels between the ending of *Perelandra* and the final cantos of Dante's *Purgatorio*.

I am thankful to a number of other scholars for providing me with the benefit of their expertise. Lewis authorities Peter Schakel, Bruce Edwards and Colin Duriez read the typescript and offered a good deal of useful commentary. My colleagues at Elizabethtown College have also been perceptive and helpful, most notably Kevin Scott in English, Anthony Matteo in philosophy, Thomas Winpenny in history and Father David Danneker in religious studies. Joy Salvatore, my research assistant at Elizabethtown, merits commendation for her thorough, intelligent and diligent work.

Research for this project has taken me a number of times to the Marion E. Wade Center at Wheaton College (Wheaton, Illinois), where I have always been impressed by the learning, professionalism and graciousness of its leaders and staff. My thanks go especially to Christopher J. Mitchell and Marjorie L. Mead for the many ways they have assisted me and so many other visiting scholars. Thanks also to Ryan Mead for his painstaking work in preparing a list of Lewis's underlinings and annotations in several books that were originally a part of Lewis's personal library.

I am grateful to my agent, Giles Anderson, for his usual good advice in shaping this project and for his good will and good faith in representing it. Thank you as well to the editorial and production teams at InterVarsity Press for their careful and conscientious work.

I count myself fortunate that members of my own family are not only among my most sympathetic readers but also among the most perceptive. Thanks to my brother Jim and my wife, Crystal, for numerous valuable suggestions on clarity and readability. My twin brother, Don, has been involved in this project from the very beginning, reading several drafts of the book. Our e-mails back and forth on the topic of mysticism run to well over a hundred pages, touching on every topic from anthroposophy to the *Zohar*. I am not surprised when mystics speak of the failure of language to convey their experience of the Divine. As for me, I don't know what words can do justice to one person's soul-deep gratitude to another.

INTRODUCTION

The Overlooked Lewis

One of the most remarkable things about C. S. Lewis, according to his friend and biographer Walter Hooper, was his singleness of heart, mind and soul. "Most Christians," Hooper explains, "seem to have two kinds of lives, their so-called 'real' life and their so-called 'religious' one. Not Lewis. The barrier so many of us find between the visible and the invisible world was just not there for him. . . . It had become natural for Lewis to live ordinary life in a supernatural way."[*]

What is it that allowed Lewis to blend so effortlessly the world of faith with the world of everyday living? How is it that, when his contemporaries were loudly proclaiming the absence of God, he was able to follow the advice of earlier thinkers for "practicing the presence of God"?

Sometimes the best clues are found in the least likely places. One such clue may appear in a letter Lewis wrote to a class of American fifth-graders concerning the Narnia Chronicles. One of them had asked if it were possible to visit Aslan's country, and Lewis replied that the only way, as far as he knew, is through death. But then he added a curious qualifier: "Perhaps some very good people get just a tiny glimpse before then."

---

[*]Source materials are listed in the notes section, arranged by page number and key words.

This is a brief remark, but a highly intriguing one. Lewis begins with that tentative "Perhaps." But who exactly are the "very good people" he has in mind? And what do they see in their "tiny glimpse"? And do they tell anyone else about it? Even this simple sentence addressed to children suggests a side of Lewis that most commentators have overlooked.

C. S. Lewis is widely regarded as the most influential voice for Christian faith in the modern era. Whether writing as a scholar, lay theologian or storyteller, he is famous for his commitment to "mere Christianity," for presenting the basic tenets of faith shared in all places at all times by Christians of the first century to those of the twenty-first.

Lewis is generally thought of as a commonsense Christian, one who offers theology that is understandable and morality that is practical. He stands in the mainstream of Christian tradition, avoiding sectarian disputes and writing for the ordinary reader.

Readers of Lewis who admire his books for their down-to-earth advice on daily living may be surprised by that brief comment of his about glimpsing Aslan's country in this life. They will probably be even more baffled by a passage in his memoir, *Surprised by Joy,* in which he describes his own conversion in overtly mystical terms: "Into the region of awe, in deepest solitude there is a road right out of the self, a commerce with . . . the naked Other, imageless (though our imagination salutes it with a hundred images), unknown, undefined, desired."

Equally unusual passages may be found in Lewis's fiction. In *That Hideous Strength,* for example, he describes a young seeker's moment of conversion not in terms of her accepting a set of beliefs or joining a church. Rather it is a moment of dramatic personal encounter:

> A boundary had been crossed. She had come into a world, or into a Person, or into the presence of a Person. Something expectant, patient, inexorable, met her with no veil or protection between. . . . In this height and depth and breadth the little idea of herself which she had hitherto called *me* dropped down and vanished, unfluttering, into bottomless distance, like a bird in a space without air.

In these passages, and many others like them, we see that the common image of Lewis as a proponent of "rational religion" does not do justice to the complexity of the man. Lewis's spiritual intuition was every bit as powerful as his intellect. For him, Christian faith was not merely a set of religious beliefs or institutional customs or moral traditions. It was rather the recognition of a profound cosmic drama, an ongoing struggle between good and evil—in unseen places, in our own workaday world and in every human heart.

Into the Region of Awe explores the often-overlooked mystical side of C. S. Lewis. It traces the mystical elements in his own life, including his lifelong experiences of what he called Joy, as well as the mystical door he envisioned in 1929 at the moment he entered into the household of faith. *Into the Region of Awe* also reveals Lewis's wide reading in Christian mystical tradition, including Augustine, Bernard of Clairvaux, Julian of Norwich as well as lesser-known works such as *The Cloud of Unknowing* and *The Scale of Perfection*. Some mystical texts Lewis later set aside as heretical or needlessly obscure, but others he quoted in his own books and recommended for meditative reading.

Generally, Lewis did not highlight his interest in Christian mysticism. He knew that many of his fellow believers misunderstood or mistrusted claims of personal encounters with the Divine, and he studiously tried to avoid topics that separate Christians, focusing instead on beliefs they can celebrate together. But a survey of Lewis's letters (some unpublished), theological meditations and works of fiction show that the spiritual vitality of his books derives in no small measure from his own mystical intuitions and from his broad reading in Christian mysticism.

Mysticism, Eastern and Western, ancient and modern, is a vast topic that could fill many volumes. In her classic study *Mysticism* (1911), Evelyn Underhill provides five hundred pages of incisive analysis and then apologizes for offering such a limited overview. Since then there have been over a hundred new books published on the subject, both from its defenders and detractors.

It is beyond the scope of this book to examine twenty centuries of

Christian mysticism.[†] Our purpose here is to examine C. S. Lewis's interest in mysticism, how it shaped his faith and contributed to his worldview. G. K. Chesterton believed that "the morbid logician seeks to make everything lucid, and succeeds in making everything mysterious. The mystic allows one thing to be mysterious, and everything else becomes lucid." Lewis was part logician, part mystic, and his books offer a unique blend of charisma and clarity—of explaining what can be known, while exploring the unknown and the unknowable.

[†]A sprightly and readable recent survey is Ursula King's *Christian Mystics: Their Lives and Legacies throughout the Ages* (Mahwah, N.J.: Hidden Spring, 2001). The most comprehensive and scholarly resource is Bernard McGinn's multivolume *The Presence of God: A History of Western Christian Mysticism* (New York: Crossroad, 1994).

~ *One* ~

THE MYSTIQUE OF
MYSTICISM

*I*n *The Perennial Philosophy* Aldous Huxley wrote that overfamiliarity with Scripture may lead to "a reverential insensibility, a stupor of the spirit, an inward deafness to the meaning of the sacred words." And surely this must be so. Otherwise Christians today could have no response but astonishment upon reading the apostle Paul's words that "we do not know how to pray as we ought, but the Spirit himself intercedes for us with sighs too deep for words" (Romans 8:26 RSV).

Does this mean that every time a harried believer offers up a halting, half-considered prayer, those words are lifted up, translated into celestial sighs, God speaking to God on our behalf? In a modern, secularized world, Christians are sometimes disparaged for taking the ancient words too literally. But do contemporary Christians believe too much or too little?

Another well-known passage whose astounding claims have been dimmed by familiarity are the apostle's words to the church at Ephesus:

> I pray that you, being rooted and established in love, may have power, together with all the saints, to grasp how wide and long and high and deep is the love of Christ, and to know this love that surpasses knowledge—that you may be filled to the measure of all the fullness of God. (Ephesians 3:17-19)

What is Paul trying to say here, and why is his language so emphatic? Is he saying his readers should affirm intellectually that Christ loves them? Or that he hopes they can imagine how important Christ's love can be? Or he trusts they will be filled with Christlike feelings of love for one another? Perhaps all these things, but surely something more. He seems to suggest that, beyond intellect, imagination or feeling, humans have a capacity to experience directly the vastness of divine love.

Christian mystics down the ages have understood St. Paul in just this sense: that all humans have a capacity to draw near to God, sometimes so near that they may apprehend directly the fullness of God in their inner being. This is a bold assertion; what sounds to some like a mere paraphrase of Paul sounds to others like zealotry and heresy. What seems to some a deeper understanding of Scripture seems to others a profound misunderstanding.

Indeed, *mysticism* may almost be defined as "that which is misunderstood." It is an elastic word, one whose precise meaning is still debated among scholars. In the popular mind the term *mysticism,* associated with the words *mystery* and even *mist,* calls forth images of clandestine societies, arcane rites and closely guarded secrets. Others identify mysticism with all things occult—astrology, Tarot cards, palmistry, séances. Still others may picture a medieval scene: a wild-eyed hermit, hollow-cheeked and threadbare, gazing in ecstasy at a luminous image that hangs in the air like a holy holograph.

None of these stereotypes conform to the great body of mystical literature or to the scholarship about mysticism. Those who look to mystical texts seeking signs and wonders are likely to be disappointed. Most Christian mystics do not see visions or hear voices. They speak rather of "the eye of the soul" or "the inner eye" by which they have experienced the divine presence.

DEFINING MYSTICISM

William James, in his classic study *The Varieties of Religious Experience* (1902), declared flatly that students of mysticism should set aside reports of clairvoyance, levitations, healings or stigmata (receiving the wounds of Christ). He defined the essential mark of a mystical state as a "consciousness of illumination." James went on to describe mystical states as

- noetic, providing a sense of new insight
- ineffable, eluding description in words
- passive, creating a sense of an overpowered will
- transitory, usually lasting two hours or less

Though Professor James was one of the first to take a "scientific" approach to mysticism, he was by no means a debunker. In fact, he concluded his study with this observation:

> Mystical states wield no authority due simply to their being mystical states. But the higher ones among them point in directions to which the religious sentiments of even non-mystical men incline. They tell of the supremacy of the ideal, of vastness, of union, of safety, and of rest. . . . The supernaturalism and optimism to which they would persuade us may, interpreted one way or another, be after all the truest of insights into the meaning of this life.

Scholar R. M. Jones agreed with James that illumination is a key element of mystical experience, but he defined the term differently. For Jones, mystical experiences do not necessarily supply new ideas to the mind; rather they transform what one believes into what one *knows,* converting abstract concepts, such as divine love, into vivid personal realities. For Jones a mystical encounter may change a person's thinking from "These are my beliefs" to "This is the Reality with which I should align myself."

By its very nature, *mysticism* eludes easy definition. Related to *mystery,* the term *mystic* is derived from Greek *myein,* "to shut," with reference either to keeping one's eyes shut or one's mouth shut. (Our word *mute* comes from the same Greek verb.) If something is by definition hidden and inexpressible, how can everyone be in on the secret?

In an oft-quoted definition, Evelyn Underhill described mysticism as "the direct intuition or experience of God." She did not think that this was a distinct faculty that some people have and others do not. Rather she insisted that "every human soul has a latent capacity for God." Mystics, for Underhill, are those who have "realized this capacity with an astonishing richness."

Underhill did not think the term *mystic* should be reserved for canonized saints who produce classic accounts of their spiritual journeys. She felt the difference between mystics and ordinary believers was their intensity of commitment. She explained the difference by saying, "This happened to them, not because God loved and attended to them more than He does to us, but because they loved and attended to Him more than we do."

Underhill also pointed out that for every well-known mystic there are myriads of anonymous ones:

> [Celebrated mystical texts] are not solitary beacons set up in the arid wilderness of "external religion." They are rather surviving records of a spiritual culture, content for the most part to live in secret, leaving few memorials behind. The stretches of country between them were inhabited by countless humble spirits, capable in their own degree of first-hand experience of God. Only realizing this can we reach a true conception of the perennial richness and freshness of the Church's inner life.

Another pioneer in the study of Christian mysticism was William R. Inge, dean of St. Paul's Cathedral in London from 1911 to 1934. Defining *mysticism* as "the experience of coming into immediate relation with the higher Powers," Inge agreed with Underhill that mystics should not be viewed as some sort of spiritual elite. He argued that the "Mystical Way" was open to all believers, that the message from earlier pilgrims is "Seek as we have sought, and you will see what we have seen."

Lewis's own definition of mysticism shows the influence of Underhill and Inge, the two most prominent British scholars on mysticism in their day. (Interestingly, Underhill was a personal acquaintance of Lewis's good friend Charles Williams, who edited a volume of her letters for Oxford University Press; Inge was close to another friend of Lewis, Adam Fox, who wrote the dean's official biography.) Lewis defined *mysticism* as a "direct experience of God, immediate as a taste or color." Noting that most mystics do not seek visions or physical manifestations, Lewis added that "There is no reasoning in it, but many would say it is an experience of the intellect—the reason resting in its enjoyment of its object."

This definition seems fairly straightforward at first, but it illustrates the difficulties that inevitably emerge in any discussion of mysticism. Taste and color are apprehended by the physical senses. With what sense is an invisible deity to be grasped? Primary sense experience is generally very difficult to put into words. Dictionaries do not define the basic colors conceptually; they simply tell you to look. A dictionary will typically define *blue* as "the color of a clear sky," *green* as "the color of growing grass" or *yellow* as "the color of a ripe lemon." These definitions are not at all helpful to a blind person, but that is the best language can do. But if words are inadequate to describe a direct sense experience such as color, how can they be of much use in describing the Absolute? As philosopher Ludwig Wittgenstein famously remarked, "If humans are incapable of describing the distinctive aroma of coffee, how can they cope with something as subtle as God?"

As if this weren't problem enough, Lewis goes on to talk about mysticism as "an experience of the intellect—the reason resting in its enjoyment of its object." Intellect and experience are usually considered contrasting modes of knowledge, what happens to you versus what you think about. One doesn't usually talk about the intellect having experiences, nor about reason enjoying.

Lewis is probably using this latter word in a technical sense that he learned from Samuel Alexander's *Space, Time, and Deity* (1924). When he first read Alexander's book, Lewis commended its "truthful antithesis of enjoyment and contemplation," that is, having an experience versus thinking about it. In choosing this word Lewis emphasizes once again that a mystical encounter is a primary, unanalyzed experience, not the product of an overly ingenious intellect or an overcharged imagination. In defining his terms Lewis was clearly aware of the problems and paradoxes that go with any discussion of this subject.

Dean Inge knew those problems only too well. At the end of his influential *Christian Mysticism* (1899), Inge offered twenty-six definitions of *mysticism,* many of them in Greek or Latin. Part of the reason he and others found the word so difficult to define is that mysticism does not refer to any one experience. Sometimes the simplest questions are the hardest ones to answer. The basic question "What is love?" calls for an answer that includes family love, romantic love, love of nature as well as teachings about the ineffable self-emptying of divine love. In the same way the question "What is mysticism?" requires some accounting for a variety of related experiences.

MYSTICAL TRANSPORT

One of the most common mystical experiences is a sense of sudden joy or transport, a glad awareness of being lifted up to grasp a higher harmony. Sometimes this moment of luminous rapture comes as the culmination of days or even years of disciplined meditation. At other times it comes unbidden, found by those who did not seek.

In his *Confessions* Augustine (354-430) eloquently described one such moment of transport: "I was caught up to Thee by thy beauty, and dragged back by my own weight, falling back once more with a groan to the world of sense. . . . I attained in the flash of one hurried glance a vision of That Which Is, but I could not sustain my gaze."

Writing seven centuries later, Bernard of Clairvaux (1090-1153) recorded a very similar experience: "Oh Sion, thou city sole and single, mystic mansions hidden in the heavens, now I rejoice in thee, now I moan for thee and mourn thee. Thee I often pass through in the heart, as I cannot in the body, for being earthly flesh and fleshly earth, soon I fall back."

These accounts from Augustine and Bernard testify to the transitory quality of the mystical moment, leaving one with a sense of paradise glimpsed but not grasped. Both also reveal that strong sense of longing which Lewis called "Sweet Desire" and which played such an important role in his own spiritual journey.

Five centuries after Bernard of Clairvaux, a brilliant French mathematician, Blaise Pascal (1623-1662), underwent what he called his "night of fire." After an indescribable experience that lasted about two hours, Pascal took out a piece of parchment and drew a cross on it, then filled the page with ecstatic, somewhat disjointed, phrases. After noting the exact date and time (10:30 p.m., Nov. 23, 1654), Pascal wrote:

Fire.
The God of Abraham, the God of Isaac, the God of Jacob.
Not of philosophers and intellectuals.
Certitude, certitude, feeling, joy, peace.
The God of Jesus Christ.
My God and Your God. [in Latin]
Your God will be my God.
Forgetfulness of the world and of everything except God.
One finds oneself only by way of directions found in the gospel.
The grandeur of the human soul.
Oh just Father, the world has not known you,
But I have known you.
Joy, joy, joy, tears of joy.

Pascal filled the rest of the page with short phrases about accepting "sweet renunciation" and never separating himself from God. Though he later wrote his *Provincial Letters* (1657), defending the doctrine of irresistible grace, and collected notes for his *Pensées,* he never told anyone about his "night of fire." When he died nine years later, a servant found the piece of parchment sewn into the lining of his jacket.

Another highly evocative account of mystical rapture is quoted in William James's *Varieties of Religious Experience:*

I remember that night, and almost the very spot on the hilltop,

where my soul opened out, as it were, into the Infinite, and there
was a rushing together of two worlds, the inner and the outer. It
was deep calling unto deep—the deep that my own struggle
opened up within being answered by the unfathomable deep without, reaching beyond the stars. I stood alone with Him who had
made me, and all the beauty of the world, and love, and sorrow,
and even temptation. I did not seek Him, but felt the perfect uni-
son of my spirit with His. The ordinary of things around me faded.
For the moment nothing but an ineffable joy and exaltation remained. The perfect stillness of the night was thrilled by a more
solemn silence. The darkness held a presence that was all the more
felt because it was not seen. . . . Never since has come quite the
same stirring of the heart. Then, if ever, I believe, I stood face to
face with God and was born anew of his spirit.

This eloquent testimony does not come from a canonized Saint but
rather an anonymous nineteenth-century saint, an obscure American
clergyman answering a questionnaire about his religious experiences. As
these last two examples show, there is nothing particularly medieval
about mysticism, nor is it reserved for those whose days are celebrated
on the church calendar.

R. M. Jones was sometimes asked how a person could tell the difference between a genuine mystical experience and a mere flight of imagination or an upsurge in religious feelings. His answer was, in part, that
if you ever had one, you would know the difference. He would sometimes explain that once while crossing the Atlantic by sea, he had a tremendous, palpable sense of being upheld by the "everlasting arms" mentioned in Deuteronomy 33:27. He felt the undeniable reality of the truth
that God is our dwelling place, his eternal arms ever sustaining us. The
day after this experience, he received a cable that his little son had died
unexpectedly. From that time on Jones felt that mysticism was not just
an academic subject but a special form of illumination that he had experienced personally.

CONTEMPLATION

Another prominent form of mysticism is disciplined meditation, what has been called "recovering the depth-life of the soul." (Scholar Nathan Söderblom calls this "cultivated mysticism," distinguishing it from "spontaneous mysticism.") For Christian mystics this is closely associated with prayer. Dean Inge declared unequivocally that every believer becomes a mystic in the act of prayer:

> But we cannot insist too strongly that the essence of mysticism— the mystical state in its purest form—is just *prayer*, "the elevation of the mind to God." Let anyone who has felt God near him when on his knees think what a perfect prayer would be like. It need not be vocal; it is probably not petitional; it is an act of worship, receptiveness, and self-surrender, to the Author of our being.

In Christian tradition a widespread desire to "practice the presence of God" has inspired a number of manuals offering advice on prayer, meditation and personal holiness. In the Middle Ages, especially, these usually followed what is called "the mystical way," a threefold process of purgation, illumination and eventual union with God. *The Dark Night of the Soul* by Spanish mystic John of the Cross (1542-1591) is this sort of manual, as are three books that C. S. Lewis studied closely: Walter Hilton's *The Scale of Perfection* (c. 1400) and two anonymous texts, *The Cloud of Unknowing* (late 1300s) and the *Theologia Germanica* (1497). Modern readers who turn to these texts expecting to find marvels, accounts of the miraculous and the supernatural, are certain to be disappointed. Medieval manuals about the mystical way focus on the soul's ascent to God, an inward, spiritual pilgrimage, not on reports of the uncanny or the unexplained.

VISIONS AND VOICES

Though less common than mystical exultation or mystical contemplation, a third type, visionary mysticism, is what often attracts the most attention. The most influential mystics—Augustine, Catherine of Siena,

John of the Cross—declared visions and voices to be peripheral, perhaps even detrimental, to one seeking an immediate, intimate awareness of God. Yet there is still a public fascination with those who exhibit extraordinary phenomena; even a rumor of "supernaturalism" seems to be more enthralling than the reality of saintliness.

Most famous of the visionaries, perhaps, is the much-beloved Francis of Assisi (1182-1226). The son of a well-to-do cloth merchant, Francis, by the age of twenty-six, had dabbled in business and played at soldiering but had done little to distinguish himself. But one day in 1208 when he was standing in the sanctuary of a dilapidated church called San Damiano, he heard a commanding voice say, "Francis, repair my church." Francis obeyed, rebuilding San Damiano stone by stone and spending the rest of his remarkable life helping repair the Church throughout thirteenth-century Europe.

While Francis did not leave any writings behind, except for his childlike "Canticle of the Sun," other well-known visionary mystics penned books full of vivid imagery and visionary theology. Teresa of Ávila is best known for her *The Interior Castle* (1577) and Jacob Boehme for *The Signature of All Things* (1623). The visionary who most influenced C. S. Lewis was Lady Julian of Norwich, the English anchorite whose *Revelations of Divine Love* (c. 1393) Lewis knew, admired and quoted often.

Raptures, contemplation, visions: these certainly are not the only expressions of mystical experience, nor are they always distinct from one another. But all seem to be part of a universal quest: the journey of the soul to ascend to the Summit of being.

IS MYSTICISM RELEVANT?

For many modern readers the first concern about mysticism is practical: is it self-indulgent, an invitation to become so heavenly minded that one is of no earthly good? With a world crying out in need, isn't it egoistic to turn one's back on others for the sake of a spiritual bubble bath?

The early Desert Fathers would have accepted the charge of escapism, for that is exactly what they were trying to do—escape the chaotic world of the Roman Empire in decline. In the third century an Egyptian, later to become St. Anthony (251?-356), chose a ruined castle on the Nile, fifty miles from the nearest city, in order to pursue private contemplation and mystical union. But as stories about his taming wild animals and battling demons grew, his followers actually journeyed to his castle and broke down a door so that they could learn from him. The desert dwellers generally barred women from their midst and many lived as hermits, refusing even to associate with other contemplatives.

But the desert hermits are the exception, not the rule. In the fifth century Augustine called the tension between action and contemplation the "Mary and Martha dilemma." Augustine noted that when Jesus visited Bethany, he told the harried hostess Martha that her sister Mary had chosen the better part in wanting to sit at his feet and listen (Luke 10:38-42). Augustine saw Martha and Mary as types of the activist and the contemplative, declaring that Mary's choice was affirmed by Jesus.

The Mary and Martha dilemma comes up often in mystical literature, usually in defense of the contemplative life against its detractors. Mystics explain that if a person is truly drawing close to God and being infused with his Spirit, then he or she will naturally mirror his character, including his unbounded love for human beings. As William Tyndale put it succinctly, "As a man feeleth God in himself, so is he to his neighbor."

In the Middle Ages it became the common wisdom that contemplation should be combined with service. As Thomas Aquinas explained in *Perfection of the Spiritual Life*:

> More is done for God by a man who suffers detriment to his beloved contemplation in order to devote himself to the salvation of his neighbor. This seems a higher perfection of love than if a man were so attached to the sweetness of contemplation that he would not give it up even when the salvation of others is at stake.

Aquinas's younger contemporary, Meister Eckhart, made the same point even more emphatically: "Even if one were in a rapture like St. Paul and there were a sick man who needed help, it would be far better to come out of the rapture and show love by serving the needy one."

Surveying Christian history, we can quickly see that many of the great mystics of the church were also its greatest leaders. The apostle Paul set the tone, referring to his being taken up to "the third heaven" (2 Corinthians 12:2) and yet working tirelessly to establish new churches among the Gentiles. Augustine, sometimes called the "Prince of Mystics," was also the bishop of Hippo as well as a prolific writer and wide traveler. Bernard of Clairvaux was founder and abbot of the monastery at Clairvaux, and one of the most influential prelates of his day. The two good friends, John of the Cross and Teresa of Ávila, together founded new Carmelite orders for men and women. As Teresa herself noted, "To give our Lord perfect service, Mary and Martha must combine."

The pattern goes on throughout church history: Francis of Assisi, Hildegard of Bingen, Catherine of Siena were all mystics but also mentors and ministers. Even in more recent times many of the great "activists" of their day—John Wesley, Florence Nightingale, Mother Teresa—have been energized not just by compassion or moral idealism but also by a mystical sense of personal mission. All of these could point to a particular life-changing moment when they felt that were called by God to a place apart.

IS MYSTICISM REAL?

However inspiring their insights, however admirable their lives, mystics inevitably evoke a basic question in the minds of modern readers: Yes, but is it real?

The first generation of modern scholars studying mysticism considered it a phenomenon of utmost theological importance. Even while recognizing certain "psycho-physical elements" in mystical experiences, Evelyn Underhill asserted that their ultimate source is the "concrete, richly living yet unchanging Reality." William R. Inge stressed the need for discernment, noting that some mystical accounts seem to be the product of unbalanced imaginations. Yet he too affirmed the theological value of authentic mystical encounters: "But some have every right to be considered as real irradiations . . . from 'the light that forever shines,' real notes of the harmony that is in immortal souls."

More recently, however, social scientists have tended to treat mysticism as a psychological topic, not a theological one. Skeptics view reported mystical raptures not as glimpses of some higher order but rather as symptoms of mental disorder.

Robert Gimello, for example, asserts that "mystical experience is simply the psychosomatic enhancement of religious beliefs and values." In reviewing the lives of some prominent mystics it is easy to see how Gimello reached this conclusion. Catherine of Siena's first vision of Christ and the apostles was said to be similar to a painting in her local church. Meister Eckhart's (c. 1260-1327) apprehension of the Absolute resembled that of some pre-Christian pantheists he was fond of reading. Mechthild of Magdeburg (c. 1210-c. 1280) had visions in which Christ appeared almost like a *minnesinger,* the German troubadours who were popular in her era.

Many mystics themselves have recognized that their spiritual visions blend divine illumination with human interpretation. And even sympathetic scholars agree that mystics do not always distinguish clearly, as St. Paul did, between what is "of the Lord" and what is self-expression (1 Corinthians 7:12, 25).

Yet when Gimello says that all mystical experiences can be explained in terms of the psychological or the physical, he is obviously leaving no room for the spiritual. In doing so he passes from psychological data to philosophical dogma. Gimello's assumption is not the kind that can be tested in a laboratory. As C. S. Lewis summarized the problem: "Science studies Nature. And the question is whether anything *besides* Nature exists, anything 'outside.' How could you find that out by studying simply Nature?"

G. K. Chesterton, the Christian apologist who greatly influenced Lewis, stated his case rather more emphatically:

Surely we cannot take an open question like the supernatural and shut it with a bang, turning the key of the madhouse on all the mystics of history. . . . You cannot take the region called the un-known and calmly say that, though you know nothing about it, you know all the gates are locked. . . . We do not know enough about the unknown to know that it is unknowable.

Apart from transcendental unknowables, we are all surrounded by a familiar unknowable: what is happening in anyone's consciousness but our own. In philosophy this is known as the "problem of other minds." We have access to our own thoughts and feelings, but have to judge everyone else's thoughts and feelings by what they say and do. When a friend says, "I was just thinking of you," he is reporting what has been happening in his private field of awareness. He has no way of proving to you that what he says is true, and you have no way of proving it is false. You have to judge the reports of others about themselves by the content of the message and by the character of the person speaking.

The task of judging mystical accounts is only the problem of other minds writ large. First, we must consider openly (not covertly, as Gimello does) whether it is even possible for a human mind to receive divine illumination not generated by our own consciousness. For those who accept the authority of the apostle Paul, this would seem not a mere possibility but an integral part of Christian living. Paul proclaims that "the Spirit himself testifies with our spirit that we are God's children" (Romans 8:16), and he refers to the work of the Spirit in our spirits more than fifty times in his epistles.

Having granted the possibility, we are free to consider individual cases on their merits. G. K. Chesterton noted that a Christian is able to investigate particular claims of the miraculous with more objectivity than a philosophical materialist. Christians believe that miracles are possible in history and in the present day, but they are under no obligation to affirm any particular claim. (This refers to miracles outside the context of Scripture, of course.) Materialists, on the other hand, are committed to naturalistic explanations and must immediately begin trying to discount all evidence to the contrary; they can't afford to admit any data that would undermine their entire worldview. As Chesterton concludes, "It is assumed that a skeptic has no bias; but he has an obvious bias in favor of skepticism."

In his essay "Transposition," C. S. Lewis discusses how events believed to be "spiritual" by people of faith may be treated as merely "psychological" by others. He gives the example of Christian mystics who use erotic imagery to portray the relation of one's soul to God. (The recurring idea of "spiritual marriage," of the soul as Christ's bride, is a commonplace in mystical literature of the medieval era.) For some readers the use of erotic imagery to describe mystical rapture may appear to be a disguised longing for more earthly raptures.

Lewis responds that in trying to explain the unknown in terms of the known, we must resort to analogy. This is especially difficult when we are trying to transpose a higher order, one that is more rich and complex, into a lower and simpler one. For example, when an orchestral symphony is transposed for a piano, the same note may have to stand for a flute in one place and a violin in another. In painting, the color white may be used for snow, a person's face or moonlight on a lake.

But if someone had never heard any instrument besides a piano, did not in fact believe there were any other instruments, how could we explain the difference in sound between a flute and a violin? Or if someone lived in the two-dimensional plane of a painting, how could we explain the use of perspective to suggest our three-dimensional world? Two-dimensional "flatlanders" might see two triangles in a painting and assume they represent the same thing. They have no way of knowing that, for those in a three-dimensional world, one triangle stands for a dunce's cap while another stands for a road stretching off to the horizon. Reductionism is the result when someone assumes that the added dimension does not actually exist, that distant roads are actually just a kind of dunce's cap.

Lewis says the critics who insist that the simpler system is the only real one will always see "all the facts, but not the meaning." They are like dogs that do not understand *pointing*. If a person points to a piece of food on the floor, most dogs will not look at the meat but sniff at the finger. For them the finger is the fact, not what it is pointing to. Lewis concludes that in an era of factual realism, people are liable to "induce upon themselves this doglike mind," always finding fresh evidence that "religion is only psychological, justice only self-protection, politics only economics, love only lust, and thought itself only cerebral biochemistry."

Of course, Lewis's remarks in "Transposition" apply to Christian belief in general, not just to mysticism. In that essay he explained the mystics' use of erotic imagery as an example of *symbolism,* explaining the unknown in terms of the known. But Lewis never offered a blanket defense of mysticism. He judged individual mystics by their fruits, finding a continuum of credibility in mystics, from resplendent holiness to regrettable heresy. On the one hand he placed the *Theologia Germanica,* Walter Hilton's *Scale of Perfection* and Julian of Norwich's *Revelations* on his short list of "great Christian books." On the other hand he quoted with approval Samuel Johnson's verdict on Jacob Boehme: "If Jacob had seen the unutterable, Jacob should not have tried to utter it."

MYSTICISM IN OTHER WORLD RELIGIONS

Lewis rejected Boehme because the latter suggested that the human soul is part of the divine soul, into which it will eventually dissolve. This sounds more like Hindu philosophy than Christian doctrine. Though Boehme was condemned by the church for heresy, his career raises another fundamental question: How does Christian mysticism fit into world mysticism at large? Most religions include mystical elements. The Jewish *Kabbalah* ("Tradition") and *Zohar* ("Splendor") include a great deal of teaching on mysticism. Islam has its Sufis, Hinduism its Yogis and Buddhism its school of Zen. If Christian mystics are drawing near to the God revealed in the Old and New Testaments, to whom (or what) are mystics from other traditions drawing near?

Rudolf Otto addressed this question when he distinguished between what he calls the "soul mysticism" of the East and the "God mysticism" of the West. Though there are exceptions, Hinduism, Buddhism and Taoism tend to stress desirable states of consciousness, escaping the fretful, self-aware state of mind that so often makes everyday living a burden. For mystics from the Abrahamic faiths, however, the inward odyssey is also an *upward* odyssey, a quest for personal and vital communion with an infinite Being.

Other Christian scholars of mysticism such as Evelyn Underhill and William R. Inge are not inclined to dismiss non-Christian mysticism. Rather they view it as a form of natural revelation, along with the order of the cosmos around us and the moral law within. They argue that all humans have an innate capacity to experience God and that members of all religious traditions can have authentic experiences of the Divine.

For one thing, Christian scholars such as Underhill, Inge and Jones, as well as humanist scholars such as William James and Aldous Huxley, all note the underlying similarities in diverse mystical traditions. To their eyes the most intriguing thing about different mystical accounts is that they are not very different. As David Baumgardt has noted, the history of science reveals later thinkers constantly overturning earlier ones, but the history of mysticism shows later mystics constantly reaffirming earlier ones. There are obvious similarities among mystical accounts from many times and places: an experience of rising above the world of the mind and the senses, of the boundaries of the self becoming blurred, of encountering the Infinite, returning with a peaceful, loving assurance of the ultimate harmony of the universe.

Despite these broad similarities, Evelyn Underhill, in particular, stresses that mysticism finds its full flowering only on the trellis of Christian tradition, particularly in the doctrines of the Trinity and the incarnation. The mystic's experience of God includes both majestic transcendence and joyous indwelling, the soul reaching out for God as God reaches into the soul. Underhill observes that Eastern mystics report experiencing God as a person, even where their religious traditions view the divine abyss as nonpersonal. Islamic mystics sense God as both far above and deep within, despite the fundamental Muslim teaching that Allah is one. Underhill concludes that only the Christian doctrines of a three-person God and an actively redemptive God provide a theological framework that adequately explains the experience of mystics the world over.

Lewis agreed with Underhill to a point—but only to a point. In "Christian Apologetics," he argues that Christians should make "clear that we are not pronouncing all other religions to be totally false, but rather saying that in Christ whatever is true in all religions is consummated and perfected." He adds the important qualifier, though, that Christians should not tolerate the "nonsensical" idea that two mutually exclusive statements about God's nature can both be true.

In the last book he wrote before his death in 1963, *Letters to Malcolm: Chiefly on Prayer,* Lewis took up the issue of non-Christian mysticism. He observes that it is becoming increasingly popular to say that mystics of all world religions are finding the same things in their quest for the Absolute. He notes the similarities of mystical experiences in different traditions but considers them a similarity of means, not ends. He agrees that all mystics undergo a temporary release from their normal time-space consciousness and logical thought processes. But he argues that the significance of mysticism lies not in this experience of emptying but rather in the filling that should follow it.

Lewis believed that even if mystical departures are similar, the true meaning of the event cannot be seen until there is an arrival: "Departures are all alike; it is the landfall that crowns the voyage." He concludes that the value of a mystical voyage depends "not at all on its being mystical—that is, on its being a departure, but on the motives, skill, and constancy of the voyager, and on the grace of God." In the Christian tradition, says Lewis, we give ear to the mystical insights of others because they are saintly; we do not consider them saintly because they report mystical experiences. As Lewis concludes, "The true religion gives value to its own mysticism; mysticism does not validate the religion in which it happens to occur."

This approach is entirely typical of Lewis. Rather than analyzing mystical states per se, he wanted to know about the character of the mystics and what insights might be derived from them. He was less interested in mystical consciousness than in its content. And, indeed, he followed some mystical voyagers very closely, exploring himself the landscapes on which they had trod.

～ *Two* ～

MYSTICAL ELEMENTS
IN LEWIS'S LIFE

C. S. Lewis did not consider himself a mystic.

In *Letters to Malcolm* Lewis said that in younger days when he took walking tours, he loved hills, even mountain walks, but he didn't have a head for climbing. In spiritual ascents he also considered himself one of the "people of the foothills," someone who didn't dare attempt the "precipices of mysticism." He added that he never felt called to "the higher level—the crags up which mystics vanish out of sight."

Despite this disclaimer, Lewis must certainly have been one of the most mystical-minded of those who never formally embarked on the mystical way. We see this in the ravishing moments of "Sweet Desire" he experienced ever since childhood, in his vivid sense of the natural order as an image of the spiritual order, in his lifelong fascination with mystical texts and in the mystical themes and images he so often appropriated for his own books. As his good friend Owen Barfield once remarked, Lewis, like George MacDonald and G. K. Chesterton before him, radiated a sense that the spiritual world is *home,* that we are always coming back to a place we have never yet reached.

AN ACHE FOR THE INFINITE

According to Rudolf Otto in *The Idea of the Holy,* one of the defining traits of the *numinous* is a habitual sense of yearning, a deep longing for something inaccessible or unknown. Throughout his lifetime Lewis had this kind of mystical yearning in abundance. In *The Problem of Pain* Lewis confesses that "all [my] life an unattainable ecstasy has hovered just beyond the grasp of [my] consciousness." Lewis was born on November 29, 1898, the second son of a successful Belfast attorney. This was the time of "the troubles" in Ireland, tensions between Catholics and Protestants that have yet to be fully resolved. Lewis's father, Albert, was a stout Ulsterman, vigorously defending the rights of the Protestants in the north of Ireland. His mother, though also Protestant, tried to stress cooperation and peaceful coexistence. Despite these contrasting temperaments, Lewis remembered his childhood home as a place of loving parents; a kind, sensible nurse; and a companionable brother, Warren, three years older.

Lewis explained years later that all during his childhood he underwent "spiritual experiences as pure and momentous" as anything he would know as an adult. These were experiences of "Joy," or "Sweet Desire," the longing for some lost paradise that is itself a kind of paradise to feel.

In his memoir *Surprised by Joy* Lewis recalls that one summer day when he was only six, there arose in him a delicious memory of an earlier time when his brother had made a toy garden, bits of twigs and moss arranged in a biscuit tin. Lewis compares the momentary sensation that came with this memory to Milton's "enormous bliss" of Eden. The experience left a permanent imprint on his imagination. It seemed to him that his brother's miniature garden was his first encounter with beauty, awakening him for the first time to the wonders of nature as something "cool, dewy, fresh, exuberant." Lewis felt that for the rest of his life his image of paradise retained something of that first childhood epiphany.

These experiences of joy recurred throughout Lewis's early years. Once it descended while he was reading Beatrix Potter's *Squirrel Nutkin* and looking at the book's pictures of leafy woods in their full autumn splendor. As happened so often, this Joy was something never quite possessed, always "over there." The pictures in the book set him to longing for the real trees outside his window, for the robust aromas and the crisp leaves crackling under his feet. But then walking among the actual trees in autumn made him long for the pictures he had seen in the book.

Another time he felt the piercing stab of Sweet Desire while reading haunting words in Longfellow about the death of the Norse god Balder. Though he had no idea at the time who Balder was, these lines filled him with the particular kind of sublime feeling he called "Northernness," a stern and ecstatic vision of things "cold, spacious, severe, pale, and remote."

The beauty of nature was also a frequent catalyst for Joy in the young Lewis. From their front door Jack (as he preferred to be called) and his brother, Warren, could look out beyond the bustling city of Belfast and see a low line of hills, cool and serene above the city of cinders. These hills on the seemingly unreachable horizon called out to him, evoking that familiar longing and ache and pleasure.

Even when he first experienced Joy as a child, Lewis recognized that the feeling was not mere nostalgia or love of nature. It was a desire, then, for what? Trying to answer that question became a kind of personal grail quest for Jack, a quest he would recount in his highly autobiographical allegory, *The Pilgrim's Regress* (1933), and again in his memoir, *Surprised by Joy* (1955). Both books are organized around the search for Joy, trying to set aside many false objects of Sweet Desire until he finally comes to rest in humble recognition of the true Object he had been seeking since childhood.

A JOYLESS BOYHOOD IN ENGLISH SCHOOLS

Lewis's happy and secure childhood came to an abrupt end in 1908 when his mother, at the age of forty-six, was diagnosed with cancer and died within seven months. Besides losing his mother, Jack in a very real sense lost his father and his home as well. Albert Lewis had always struggled with an uncertain temper, and his grieving over his lost wife tended to drive others away rather than draw them closer. The anguished time of Mrs. Lewis's decline and death set a pattern of strained relations between Jack and his father that would persist for over two decades until

1929, when Albert fell into his own last illness.

Less than a month after the death of their mother, Jack and Warren were sent to Wynyard, a boarding school in Watford, England. As if the two brothers were not already suffering enough, this turned out to be a wretched place run by a brutal, mentally unbalanced schoolmaster. Wynyard had only one classroom and one dormitory, no library, laboratory or athletic fields. The sickroom doubled as a storage room and the stench from the outdoor toilets often permeated the whole facility.

Part of the regimen at Wynyard was mandatory attendance at a nearby church with high Anglican services. As an Ulster Protestant the young Lewis initially detested this church as too "Romish," but he was eventually impressed by the earnestness with which Christian doctrines were expounded there. Lewis later said he first came to serious faith at that time. But unfortunately this newfound belief did not provide him with assurance or comfort but rather created self-condemnation. He fell into an internalized legalism, such that his private prayers never seemed good enough. He felt his lips were saying the right things, but his mind and heart were not in the words.

Lewis later explains in *Surprised by Joy* that his boyhood faith was weighed down by the "ludicrous burdens of false duties in prayer." Lewis adds, "If only someone had read to me old Walter Hilton's warning that we must never in prayer strive to extort 'by maistry' [mastery] what God does not give." This is one of those casual references in Lewis that reveals a whole other side to him which may surprise those who think of him mainly as a Christian rationalist.

"Old Walter Hilton" is the fourteenth-century author of a manual for contemplatives called *The Scale of Perfection*. This book is sometimes called *The Ladder of Perfection,* as it presents the image of a ladder upon which one's soul may ascend to a place of perfect unity and rest in the Spirit of God. (The scale referred to in the Latin title, *Scala Perfectionis,* is a device for climbing, a scaling ladder, not a device for weighing.)

The passage about the "maistry" Lewis wished he had known as a boy comes early in *The Scale of Perfection,* a section about different kinds of prayer, including liturgical prayers, spontaneous prayers and "prayers in the heart alone," which do not use words. Hilton's advice for people "who are troubled by vain thoughts in their prayer" is not to feel alone. He notes it is very common to be distracted in prayer by thoughts of what "you have done or will do, other people's actions, or matters hindering or vexing you." He explains that no one can keep fully the Lord's command to love the Lord your God with all your heart, soul, strength and mind. The best you can do is humbly acknowledge your weakness and ask for mercy. However badly your first resolve fades, says Hilton, you should not get "too fearful, too angry with yourself, or impatient with God for not giving you savor and spiritual sweetness in devotion." Instead of feeling wretched it is better to leave off and go do some other good or useful work, resolving to do better next time. Hilton concludes that even if you fail in prayer a hundred times, or a thousand, God in his charity will reward you for your labor.

Walter Hilton was the canon of a priory in the Midlands of England and an experienced spiritual director of those who had taken monastic vows. His book is full of mellow wisdom about spiritual growth, and Lewis considered it one of the "great Christian books" that is too often neglected by modern believers. Hilton's recurring theme—do what you know to be right and don't worry about your feelings—is one that appears often in Lewis's own Christian meditations.

But, alas, Lewis as a boy did not have the benefit of Hilton's advice. In those boyhood years at Wynyard he was trapped in a religion of guilt, not grace. More and more he came to associate Christianity with condemnation of others, as in the north of Ireland, or condemnation of oneself for not living up to God's standards.

When he was in his early teens Lewis decided to put away childish things, including his faith. After leaving Wynyard he spent a term at Campbell College, near his home in Belfast, then traveled to Cherbourg House, a private boarding school in Worcestershire. At Cherbourg Lewis became acquainted with occult philosophies such as Rosicrucianism as well as other world religions besides Christianity. Before long he decided that Christianity was only one religion among many, and not necessarily the most compelling. He set aside his childhood faith not with regret but relief. For him the burden that needed to roll away was not sin but rather fear and self-accusation.

After Cherbourg House, Lewis moved on to Malvern, a preparatory school in the same town. Since he was intensely unhappy there, his father eventually arranged to have him study with a private tutor in Great Bookham, Surrey. Living with this outspokenly atheistic tutor, William Kirkpatrick, Lewis found his unbelief reinforced by his reading in the natural sciences and the social sciences. From the former he gained a sense that life on earth is just a random occurrence in a vast, empty universe, that all of human history is no more than a teardrop in the vast ocean of eternity. From the latter he concluded that all the world's religions, including Christianity, could be best explained not as claims to truth but as expressions of psychological needs and cultural values.

From his early teens to his late twenties Lewis entertained a series of worldviews, from philosophical materialism to dualism to idealism, before he began to seriously reconsider Christianity. Especially during his teens Lewis lived daily with what he described later as an almost unendurable paradox: "Nearly all that I loved I believed to be imaginary; nearly all that I believed to be real I thought grim and meaningless."

AN EARLY MILESTONE: GEORGE MACDONALD

Despite his intellectual skepticism during those years, Lewis never lost his sense of wonder, a certain mystical intuition that there was more to the story than his rational side could find. If his reason had truly reigned, he would have quickly dismissed anything written by George Mac-Donald, the nineteenth-century Scottish homilist, poet and fantasy writer. But when Lewis, at age seventeen, discovered MacDonald's *Phantastes,* it was an emotional and spiritual watershed. Reading the story for the first time in the spring of 1916, Lewis wrote enthusiastically to a friend that he had a "great literary experience" that week, and the book became one of his lifelong favorites. Over a decade later Lewis wrote that nothing gave him a sense of "spiritual healing, of being washed" as much as reading George MacDonald.

Phantastes (1858) is an episodic, dreamlike book, rich with mystical overtones. It tells the story of a young man named Anodos, literally "one who has lost his way," whose adventures in fairy country bring him into a fuller harmony with the world of nature and help him discover in himself a "capacity for simple happiness" that he had never felt before. After his adventures in fairy country, including even his seeming death, Anodos returns to his own world feeling that he has indeed found his way, that he has acquired "a power of calm endurance" that he had hitherto not known.

Phantastes is a singular and peculiar tale, sometimes disjointed in plot and uneven in style. But whatever its oddities *Phantastes* was for Lewis a great balm to the soul, not only in his youth but throughout his lifetime. In his preface to the MacDonald anthology he edited two decades later, Lewis wrote that he "crossed a great frontier" when he first read *Phantastes,* that the book had "a sort of cool, morning innocence" about it, which helped baptize his imagination.

Looking back, Lewis in later years did not mistake this kind of baptism for conversion itself, yet he recognized it as the beginning of a long process. As he explained, *Phantastes* "did nothing to my intellect nor (at that time) my conscience. Their turn came far later and with the help of many other books and men. But when the process was complete, . . . I found that I was still with MacDonald and that he had accompanied me all the way." Only after that process was complete could Lewis fully explain what was so compelling in that first reading: "The quality which had enchanted me in his imaginative works turned out to be the quality of the real universe, the divine, magical, terrifying, and ecstatic reality in which we all live."

Though he didn't recognize it at the time, the young Lewis was responding warmly to the Christian mysticism that pervades all of MacDonald's writing. Lewis later called MacDonald a "mystic and natural symbolist who was seduced into writing novels." This judgment is borne

out by critic Rolland Hein in summarizing the worldview which under-
lies MacDonald's fiction. Tracing the influence of Novalis (1772-1801),
Hein finds in MacDonald a pervasive quest to find "an inner harmony
commensurate with the harmony seen in the outer universe" as well as
a "yearning after the eternal and the infinite—a type of spiritual love
which draws man toward the divine."

Hein also notes that "MacDonald felt deeply the great possibility for
mankind to grow into complete godlikeness, so that men shall be one
with God. This does not mean that men shall be absorbed into God, as
pantheism holds, but that as men mature into moral and spiritual perfection, they develop at the same time a more distinct individuality."
With more gender-inclusive language this summary could serve as an
apt description of the mystic way, as set forth by Walter Hilton, Teresa of
Ávila or John of the Cross.

WAR AND MRS. MOORE

Lewis entered University College, Oxford, in April 1917, but his education was soon interrupted by a two-year stint in the British army during
World War I. In June 1917 he joined a cadet battalion billeted in Oxford,
where his roommate was Edward F. C. "Paddy" Moore. The two soon became friends, and Paddy introduced Jack to his mother, Mrs. Janie King
Moore, then forty-five, and his eleven-year-old sister Maureen.

Before they were shipped off to France, Jack and Paddy pledged to
each other that if one of them did not return from the fighting, the other
would do his best to look after the parent left behind. Jack arrived at the
frontlines on his nineteenth birthday, November 29, 1917. In February
of the following year he developed a case of trench fever and spent a
month in a French hospital. Then in April he was wounded in three
places by an English shell that fell short. He had to be evacuated first to
a mobile hospital in France and then back to England.

In that same spring of 1918 Paddy was reported missing in action and
confirmed as dead by the end of the summer. During his convalescence
Jack was never able to convince his father Albert, still in Belfast, to visit

him in an English hospital. Yet Mrs. Moore came often; the bereaved mother and the abandoned son turned to each other for strength and consolation. During that time Lewis in effect exchanged parents, gaining a new mother but losing a father. When Jack returned to Oxford in 1919 to resume his studies, he finished out his last year of required residence, then moved in with Maureen and Mrs. Moore. Before long he began introducing her as his mother, and the two stayed together for over thirty years until her death in 1951.

It was indirectly, through Mrs. Moore, that Lewis underwent a harrowing experience in the spring of 1923 that permanently influenced his spiritual outlook. While studying with Kirkpatrick before the war, he had developed what he called a "penchant for mystical philosophy," by which he meant an interest in the paranormal and the occult. This fascination lasted for several years as he read books on ghosts and visions, conjuring, spiritualism, and sorcery. This interest was dampened when he met several actual spiritualists in Oxford after the war. And it was utterly extinguished when a close acquaintance of his, Mrs. Moore's brother John, who had dabbled heavily in the occult, suffered a complete psychic collapse. From 1923 onward Lewis resolved he would henceforth stick to "the beaten track, the approved road" (see p. 151).

In later years Lewis found a great deal of philosophical significance in his youthful flirtation with what he called Magic. But the immediate effect was a sense that spiritual realities were less remote, less hypothetical, than he had previously believed. Good and evil began to seem less philosophical postulates than unseen spiritual forces. Later on, Lewis did not say his youthful interest in the occult was dangerous or deceptive; he says more emphatically that it was a stratagem of "the Enemy."

Having lived with a "divided mind" in his teens and early twenties, Lewis's intellect, imagination and spiritual intuitions began to coalesce in his mid- to late twenties. He completed his Oxford studies with great distinction, earning First Class degrees in classics (1920), ancient philosophy (1922) and English literature (1923). In the 1924-1925 academic year Lewis accepted a one-year appointment as a lecturer and tutor in philosophy, a position that afforded him the opportunity for broad and careful reading in philosophy, from ancient to modern.

During this time Lewis embraced Idealism, the philosophy that the world of the senses is but an appearance and that ultimate reality is a transempirical Absolute, "the fuller splendor behind the sensuous curtain." But the more he tried to live out this worldview, the more it seemed to him that the Absolute had to be something more than a transcendent Ground of Being. He sensed, perhaps more by intuition than intellect, that he was grappling with something—or Someone—concrete and personal. As he wrote to his friend Owen Barfield in a tone of humorous panic, "Terrible things are happening to me. The 'Spirit' or 'Real I' is showing an alarming tendency to become much more personal and is taking the offensive, and behaving just like God. You'd better come on Monday at the latest or I may have entered a monastery."

MYSTICAL ELEMENTS IN LEWIS'S CONVERSION

In his memoir *Surprised by Joy* (1955) Lewis described two conversion experiences, the first to a generalized theism, the second to Christianity specifically, an affirmation that Jesus of Nazareth was God come down from heaven. The first of these was a mystically charged experience that occurred in the summer of 1929. Having affirmed that there is an Absolute, Lewis was increasingly attracted to Christians he had met at Oxford, especially J. R. R. Tolkien, and to Christian authors he had been reading, especially Samuel Johnson, George MacDonald and G. K. Chesterton. Then one summer's day, riding on the top deck of an omnibus, he became aware, without words or clear mental pictures, that he was "holding something at bay, or shutting something out." He felt he was being presented with a free choice, that of opening a door or bolting it shut. He said he felt no weight of compulsion or duty, no threats or rewards, only a vivid sense that "to open the door . . . meant the incalculable."

Lewis chose to open the door and the consequences seemed not only incalculable but almost ineffable. Writing in *Surprised by Joy* more than a quarter century later, Lewis struggled to find the right metaphor to capture the experience. In the short space of one paragraph he describes the moment as walking through a door, but also like taking off a tight corset, removing one's armor and even the melting of a snowman. Obviously something profound and pivotal happened that day, but trying to do it justice seemed to push Lewis to the outer reaches of his considerable expressive powers.

After the experience on the bus Lewis took a full two years trying to figure out what it meant. He began by kneeling and praying soon afterwards, "the most dejected and reluctant convert in all England." Then he started to explore a variety of spiritual and mystical texts. Though there are only scattered references to "devotional" reading in Lewis's letters or diaries in his twenties, the two-year period 1929-1931 found him reading George MacDonald's *Diary of an Old Soul* and *Lilith,* John Bunyan's *Grace Abounding,* Dante's *Paradiso,* Jacob Boehme's *The Signature of All Things,* Brother Lawrence's *The Practice of the Presence of God,* Thomas Traherne's *Centuries of Meditations,* William Law's *An Appeal to All Who Doubt* and Thomas à Kempis's *Imitation of Christ,* as well as the Gospel of John in the original Greek.

All this thinking and reading came to a head in September 1931, when Lewis was persuaded by J. R. R. Tolkien and another Christian friend that Christ's incarnation is the historical embodiment of the dying god myth, the universal story of One who gives himself for the sake of his people. Lewis's second conversion, his acknowledgment that Christ is God, once again came while riding, this time in the sidecar of his brother Warren's motorcycle.

Of all the texts Lewis read during his spiritual apprenticeship, one that affected him the most was the Gospel of John (in Greek), which he said made all other religious writing seem like a comedown. He also responded strongly to Jacob Boehme's *The Signature of All Things* (1623). On his first reading of it in 1930, Lewis said it had been "about the biggest shaking up I've got from a book since I first read *Phantastes*." After talking about qualities of horror and dread, which made Boehme less pleasant than MacDonald, Lewis concludes, "It's not like a book at all, but like a thunderclap. Heaven defend us—what things there are knocking about in the world!" Part of what filled Lewis with uneasy fascination was Boehme's portrayal of God when there was nothing but God. The book of Genesis begins with God in the act of creation. But Boehme goes back a step and describes "the eternal Stillness," a no-place and no-time with only the infinite Being and Non-Being. Perhaps more importantly, Lewis encountered in Boehme the first fully articulated system of nature mysticism.

Jacob Boehme (1575-1624) was a German shoemaker who began having visions while still a boy. From his personal revelations Boehme developed a philosophy that he considered an enrichment of Christianity but which church authorities condemned as heretical. For Boehme, nature is truly the garment of God, as all natural things are symbols of spiritual things. Boehme was well versed in alchemy, focusing especially on quicksilver (mercury), salt and sulfur. For him quicksilver was a symbol of human consciousness and salt a sign of immortality because of its preservative qualities. Sulfur was a material that when ignited vaporized into "sulfur spirits." This made it a mystical symbol of a soul inhabiting a body. For Boehme all material things have a "signature," an essential quality by which to read the nature of spiritual things.

Jacob Boehme's works were condemned for their seemingly pantheistic teaching that human souls partake of the Universal Soul. Yet his philosophy echoed down the centuries, an important influence in thinkers as diverse as the American Transcendentalists, the British Theosophists and German Romantics such as Novalis. Another latter-day reader of Boehme was George MacDonald, who expressed his nature mysticism in sacramental terms. "What on God's earth," asks a character in MacDonald's novel *The Portent,* "is *not* an outward and visible sign of an inward and spiritual grace?" MacDonald's son Greville recalled later that his father spoke of *correspondences,* "innumerable instances of physical law tallying with metaphysical, of chemical affinities with spiritual affections."

Lewis's early letters show an equal enthusiasm for Boehme and for his more orthodox disciple George MacDonald. Lewis's friend and biographer, George Sayer, observed that Jack's view of nature was "essentially mystical" and that he spoke of nature as "the signature of all things." Lewis dropped Boehme's alchemy and justified his views instead with St. Paul's observation that "since the creation of the world God's invisible qualities—his eternal power and divine nature—have been clearly seen, being understood from what has been made" (Romans 1:20).

For Lewis, nature mysticism was not so much a philosophy as a deeply realized sense of joy and gratitude in the beauty of the natural world. He liked all kinds of weather and loved to fill his letters with minute descriptions of landscapes, farmyards, forests, skies, storm clouds and sunsets. He often made explicit the spiritual resonances he saw in the natural world. In one letter he compares the woods at Whipsnade Zoo, with their bluebells and birdsongs, to "the world before the Fall." In another he says that early morning luminosity of a country churchyard before Easter service "makes the Resurrection seem almost *natural*."

Sometimes in his letters Lewis drew out more fully the spiritual lessons to be learned at the feet of nature. For example, he mused that "the whole business of life, the only road to love and peace, the cross and the crown in one . . . is but unimpeded obedience." He adds that we find the natural world so beautiful and restful because all things there "unswervingly carry out the will of their Creator." He thought that was why the Romantics so often felt "a certain holiness in the wood and water." Their pantheistic leanings may have been misguided, but their feeling was just. And Christians can enjoy the same feeling with a better sense of what it means.

In another letter Lewis explains St. James's description of God as "the Father of lights" in Boehmian terms: "He is pure Light. All the *heat* that in us is lust or anger in Him is cool light—eternal morning, eternal freshness, eternal springtime: never disturbed, never strained. Go out in early summer before the world is awake and see, not the thing itself, but the material symbol of it."

In *Mere Christianity* Lewis goes beyond momentary impressions and gives an account of everything in the cosmos as a mirror of God's nature. Space, in its very immensity, is a symbol of God's greatness, a "translation of it into non-spiritual terms." The physical energy in matter reminds us of the spiritual power of God. Growing plant life is a sign of the living God, as animal life is a sign of his ceaseless activity and creative power. And humans, in their ability to think and will and love, are the most complete and fully realized image of God in this earthly realm.

Lewis himself seemed to feel that his intense response to nature went beyond mere aesthetic enjoyment to what many would consider a variety of mystical experiences. In *The Problem of Pain* he confesses, "There have been times when I think we do not desire heaven; but more often I find myself wondering whether, in our heart of hearts, we have ever desired anything else." He goes on to talk about a "secret thread" that ties together all the books he loves the most. Then there is the view of a landscape "which seems to embody what you have been looking for all your life," even if a friend standing nearby "cares nothing for the ineffable suggestion by which you are transported." Adding that even a person's friendships and hobbies are shaped by this hunger in the heart, Lewis concludes, "All the things that have ever deeply possessed your soul have been just hints of it—tantalizing glimpses, promises never quite fulfilled, echoes that died away just as they caught your ear." Lewis adds that if the object of this yearning were ever made manifest, we could say, beyond all doubt, "Here at last is the thing I was made for." He calls this "the secret signature of each soul, the incommunicable and unappeasable want."

In using terms such as *ineffable, transport* and *signature of the soul,* Lewis is clearly adopting the vocabulary of mysticism to describe his own soul's deepest longings. Mysticism scholar W. T. Stace distinguishes between "introverted mysticism," based on meditation or contemplation, and "extroverted mysticism," an ecstatic response to visible emblems of the "First Fair" found in nature. Clearly, Lewis's mysticism is mainly of the second sort.

KINDRED SPIRITS AT OXFORD
Lewis's mystical side was nourished not only by his reading and by the natural world but also by like-minded spirits in his own life. In 1933

Lewis humorously dubbed his literary circle the Inklings, taking the name from a defunct undergraduate club. Meeting Thursday evenings in Lewis's rooms at Magdalen College, where he had been elected a Fellow in 1925, they read their compositions aloud and offered each other frank, if friendly, critiques. Soon Tuesday morning meetings in a local pub were added, where, in any given week, it might include Jack's brother Warren, J. R. R. Tolkien, Colin Hardy, Humphrey Havard as well as Owen Barfield or Hugo Dyson whenever they were in Oxford.

In the autumn of 1939 Charles Williams moved to Oxford and quickly became a regular at Inklings meetings. He worked for the London branch of Oxford University Press, which moved out of the capital during World War II. Lewis had read Williams's "supernatural thriller" *The Place of the Lion* in 1936 and sent him a congratulatory note just as Williams was getting ready to write Lewis to tell him how much he admired Lewis's scholarly achievement in *The Allegory of Love.* When Williams moved to Oxford, he and Lewis became devoted friends.

Born in 1886, Charles Williams was a prolific writer as well as an energetic lecturer and editor. He is probably best known for his seven novels of the supernatural, which one critic described as "wild and mystical." But he also wrote plays, book-length Arthurian poems, literary commentaries and two classic short meditations on theology and church history, *He Came Down From Heaven* (1938) and *The Descent of the Dove* (1939).

Lewis and Williams valued each other's company partly because the two of them had few intellectual equals. But they also shared the same vivid sense of spiritual realities just beyond the doors of perception. T. S. Eliot, who said he considered Williams very nearly a saint, commented that "he makes our everyday world much more exciting because of the supernatural which he always finds active in it." This sounds very much like George Sayer describing Lewis: "The most precious moments to Jack in his ordinary life were those . . . when he was aware of the spiritual quality of material things, of the infusion of the supernatural into the workaday world."

The central thread of Williams's thought, and the one that most influenced Lewis, is his idea of "Co-inherence." Williams believed that coinherence is built into the very fabric of reality, a reflection of the Trinity: Father, Son and Holy Spirit, three persons in one being, eternally expressing their natures in relation to the others. Coinherence leads to substitution, Christ's dying for all humanity in order that they may be lifted up. Redeemed humans coinhere in their Maker, living in the Spirit as he lives in them, and also with each other in a mystical body.

For Williams coinherence was not just a theological abstraction but a practical relation. He believed that Paul's advice to bear one another's burdens (Galatians 6:2) was more than just a call for mutual aid or emotional support. He taught that a Christian could actually accept someone else's physical, emotional or spiritual burdens, to reenact Christ's substitution by taking upon oneself the dread, pain or anxiety of another.*

Williams even suggested that such a substitution could transcend time. In his novel *Descent into Hell* (1937) a young, modern-day woman sees a vision of one of her ancestors being martyred for his faith in the sixteenth century. She senses his terrible agony in facing death and takes a portion of his suffering on herself. In so doing she finds a peace that had eluded her, while her ancestor goes forward to his death proclaiming, "I have seen the salvation of my God."

When asked in a letter about Williams's ideas of coinherence and substitution, Lewis responded that he would not argue against them. He noted that Jesus asks Saul on the road to Damascus, "Why do you persecute *me?*" not "Why do you persecute my followers?" Lewis takes this to mean that "our Lord suffers in all the sufferings of His people." He goes on to speculate that "when we suffer for others and offer it to God

---

*New Testament scholar F. F. Bruce finds this teaching implied by the apostle Paul himself in his epistles. Bruce comments that Paul "seems to have believed that the more of these sufferings he personally absorbed, the less would remain for his fellow-Christians to endure." Quoting from Colossians 1:24, 2 Corinthians 1:6 and 2 Corinthians 4:12, Bruce concludes: "As Jesus had offered up to God the injuries inflicted on him as an atonement 'for many,' so Paul accepted his injuries and trials the more readily in the hope that . . . fellow-believers would be spared the like" (Bruce, p. 69).

on their behalf, it may be united with His sufferings and, in Him, may help to their redemption."

Williams reinforced Lewis's mystical side not only in life but also in his death. When Williams died unexpectedly in 1945, Lewis was deeply saddened but somehow also sustained. In later years, speaking of the strong sense of Presence he felt after his good friend's passing, Lewis wondered if God welcomed souls newly arrived in the "City of Grace" with a power to bless those left behind. As he observed in 1946, "No event has so corroborated my faith in the next world as Williams did simply by dying. When the idea of death and the idea of Williams thus met in my mind, it was the idea of death that was changed."

LATE LOVE AND LOSS

Lewis biographer George Sayer says that Williams found a special place in Lewis's heart, a place that would not be filled again until he met Joy Davidman. She was an American poet and novelist who was a Marxist in her youth but who later converted to Christianity, partly through reading Lewis's books. Davidman, then Mrs. Bill Gresham, began exchanging correspondence with Lewis in 1950, and the two met for the first time in Oxford in 1952.

Joy had a bluff, hearty, no-nonsense manner, which Lewis once clumsily complimented as her "masculine virtues." ("How would you like me to compliment you on your feminine virtues?" was her trenchant reply.) But despite her incisive intellect, Joy also had a mystical side. All her life she remembered something that happened to her as a fourteen-year-old: her sense of epiphany in watching a sunset through the glistening, ice-glazed branches of a tree. Though her atheist Jewish father felt the experience could easily be explained away, she retained a sense that somehow she'd witnessed a kind of burning bush.

Many years later Joy told Jack about another experience she'd had as a new Christian, before she met him. She was "haunted all one morning" by an intuitive sense of the nearness of God, that he was demanding her attention. She tried to ignore the feeling, afraid this was a matter of some unrepented sin or unwanted labor. But when she finally acknowledged the Presence, as Lewis explains it, "the message was, 'I want to give you something' and instantly she entered into joy."

When Lewis met Joy in 1952, her marriage was under severe strain. By the end of 1953 a breakup seemed inevitable, and she moved to England with her two sons. Joy was divorced from Gresham, and gradually her friendship with Lewis deepened into something more than friendship. When the English Home Office refused to extend Joy's visa in 1955, Lewis agreed to marry her in a civil ceremony in order to give her English citizenship. Some of Lewis's closest friends objected to this, but he felt, perhaps naively, that a civil ceremony was a mere formality that would not affect their actual relationship.

In October 1956 Joy was diagnosed with bone cancer. The news seems to have changed her relationship with Lewis; within a few months it was clear their companionship had ripened into love. The two were married in an Anglican ceremony in her hospital room in March 1957. By then Joy's cancer was in an advanced stage; she was confined to bed in a great deal of pain. When she was released from the hospital in April, it was assumed she had only weeks to live.

At that time Lewis began praying that he could be a substitute for his wife, that he could accept some of her pain and debility. That summer and fall Joy's cancer went into remission, and the bone tissue in her thigh began to mend. At the same time Lewis experienced crippling pain in his legs as well as loss of calcium in his bones. He told several friends that he couldn't help but wonder if Williams's mystical idea of substitution were not valid indeed.

Mr. and Mrs. Lewis had a wonderful "Indian summer" together in her last years; she became strong enough to walk and eventually travel with Jack to Ireland in the summer of 1958. By the autumn of 1959 the bone cancer returned and Jack wrote that the "wonderful recovery Joy made in 1957 was only a reprieve not a pardon." Despite her deteriorating condition, they traveled to Greece in the spring of 1959 with their friends Roger and June Lancelyn Green. Lewis wrote a friend soon afterward that Joy had been "divinely supported" during the trip, in which she had realized "beyond hope, her greatest, lifelong, this-worldly desire." Joy Davidman Lewis died in July 1960 at forty-five years old.

Jack's own health was not good in the years following Joy's death. He suffered from heart and kidney disease and began receiving blood transfusions in 1961. He had a heart attack in July 1963 and went into a coma. After receiving last rites, he surprised everyone by waking up from his coma and asking for a cup of tea. Though he was comfortable and cheerful, Lewis never fully recovered from this condition. He died quietly on November 22, 1963.

Considering Lewis's adolescent interest in conjuring apparitions, it seems ironic that he himself should experience such a vision, unbidden, in the last months of his life. Walter Hooper reports that one afternoon during Lewis's hospitalization in July, he suddenly pulled himself up and stared intently across the room. He seemed to gaze at something or someone "very great and beautiful" near at hand, for there was a rapturous expression on his face unlike anything Hooper had seen before. Jack kept on looking, and repeated to himself several times, "Oh, I never imagined, I never imagined." The joyous expression remained on his features as he fell back onto his pillows and went to sleep. Later on, he remembered nothing of this episode, but he said that even speculating about it with Hooper gave him a "refreshment of the spirit."

There is little doubt that such an experience was related to Lewis's serious medical condition. Nonetheless, it seems fitting that for once, fleetingly, the "unattainable ecstasy" he'd been seeking his whole life was something to be grasped, an assurance of things unseen.

Rudolf Otto wrote that Christianity is not a mystical religion, because it is not built on private intuitions. Rather he calls it a historical faith with "mystical coloring." Perhaps Otto's description of Christian tradition may fit individual Christians as well. Though Lewis did not claim to be a mystic, his faith always displayed a distinct mystical coloring, an iridescence of rich and glittering hues.

~ *Three* ~

CHRISTIAN MYSTICISM

AS LEWIS KNEW IT

*I*n all times and places there have been those who seek to escape the bonds of flesh and ascend to be united with God. In Christian teaching, God descended into flesh in order to make that union possible. This gives a unique character to Christian mysticism, the only religion whose founder is believed to be God himself come to earth and with whom followers may still enter into communion.

Lewis knew the Bible thoroughly and read widely in the tradition of Christian mysticism. His reading was more personal than professional, so he tended to overlook what most scholars would consider major figures such as Meister Eckhart and Hildegard of Bingen. But he returned over and over to certain favorites, especially English mystics such as Walter Hilton and Julian of Norwich. Lewis's interest in reported encounters with the Divine extended from the earliest books of the Bible all the way to Christian mystics of his own generation, such as Simone Weil and Sundar Singh.[*]

---

[*]Readers familiar with Eastern Orthodox mysticism may be surprised to find no discussion here of major figures such as Maximus the Confessor (c. 580-662), John Climacus (c. 570-c. 649), Symeon the New Theologian (949-1022) or Gregory of Palamas (c. 1296-1359). But this chapter necessarily focuses on Christian mysticism as Lewis knew it, and his familiarity with the Eastern Orthodox tradition was limited.

THE OLD TESTAMENT

The tradition of Christian mysticism finds its roots in passages throughout the Bible. In the Old Testament, God reveals himself in a series of
theophanies, manifestations to humans such as the burning bush that
awed Moses (Exodus 3) or the "still small voice" that spoke to Elijah (1
Kings 19:12 KJV). Equally well known is the vision of Isaiah in which he
saw the Lord of hosts attended by seraphs, who cried, "Holy, holy, holy
is the LORD Almighty; / the whole earth is full of his glory." These seraphs
had three pairs of wings: one to fly, one to cover their feet and one to hide
their faces from his glory. Isaiah thought he was undone, a man of un-
clean lips, till one of the seraphim touched the prophet's mouth with a
live coal to purge away his sin (Isaiah 6).

In the literature of Christian mysticism Old Testament theophanies
are referred to often, and they provide a great deal of the imagery found
in later visionary texts. For Lewis as well these are among the passages
that stood out in his mind, not simply as classic accounts of divine
epiphanies but also as symbols for later believers to describe their experience of God. For example, in *Letters to Malcolm* he talks about how easily we forget that the world is "big with God," that "all ground is holy and
every bush (could we but perceive it) a Burning Bush." He adds that in
the highest forms of prayer we recover an awareness that "here is the
holy ground; the Bush is burning now." (Lewis may well have derived
this idea from Julian of Norwich, who proclaimed that in her moments
of illuminated vision, "every common bush was afire with God.")

In discussing the impact of the Bible on English literature, Lewis lists
Elijah's discovering God in a "still small voice" as one of the incidents
that will speak most fully to readers who are Christian by conviction or
Romantic by temperament. In *Miracles* Lewis discusses the danger of describing God too pantheistically, as a vast, calm ocean or a dome of radiant light. He notes that those who have approached God most closely report a "still small voice," not a sense of emptiness or a vast silence. He
adds that "the stillness in which mystics approach Him is intent and

alert," that "the ultimate Peace is silent through very density of life. Saying is swallowed up in being."

Lewis offers vivid reworkings of Isaiah's vision both in his nonfiction and fiction. He ends *The Problem of Pain* on a soaring note, a rapturous blend of theology and poetry. Having begun the book describing how the vastness of the universe makes humans feel utterly inconsequential, he reinterprets that same vastness at the end as a mystic metaphor of God's infinite grandeur. He describes God as "the abyss of self-existing Being" beyond anything humans or angels can conceive or imagine: "All thrones and powers and mightiest of the created gods . . . cover their eyes from the intolerable light of utter actuality, which was and is and shall be, which never could have been otherwise, which has no opposite." In the closing pages of *The Voyage of the "Dawn Treader,"* as the seafarers near the World's End, they witness a solemn and dramatic ritual in which an old man with a long, silver beard sings to the rising sun. Thousands of great, white birds fly out from the direction of the dawn, and one places a glowing berry, like a live coal, in the old man's mouth. He is Ramandu, a once and future star, who will rejoin the "great dance" of the cosmos once the fire berries he tastes every morning have given him back his youth. In this numinous episode Lewis calls to mind Isaiah's vision of a seraph who touches the prophet's lips with a live ember in order to make him whole.

Apart from Old Testament passages that portray God in terms of his sovereignty and majesty, mystics down the ages have also cherished those books which most fully express a deep personal longing for God. Not surprisingly, passages from Psalms appear more often than any other book of the Bible in mystical texts. (Psalms is also the one book of the Bible to which Lewis devoted an entire monograph, *Reflections on the Psalms*.)

Perhaps more surprising are the frequent references in mystical literature to the Song of Songs. Though the love poetry found in that book is not mystical in itself, it has been read since the time of the early church fathers as an allegory of the soul's relation to God. One of the most oft-quoted phrases from the Song of Songs is taken from Song 5:2:

"I sleep, but my heart waketh" (KJV). In the third century after Christ, Origen interpreted the phrase symbolically: even when our minds are upon earthly things, the "spark of the soul" seeks and longs for the things of heaven.

Of course, Lewis was well acquainted with this tradition. Once when a friend and former student of his, Martin Moynihan, said he was having trouble reading a Latin inscription on a grave that began, *"Ego dormio,"* Lewis completed the phrase, *"Ego dormio sed cor meum vigilat."* He translated it to mean, "I sleep, but my heart watcheth," and explained the context from the Song of Songs. Moynihan later wrote that those same words might serve as a fitting epitaph for Lewis himself: the Latin phrase may also be translated, "I sleep, but my soul wakes."

THE NEW TESTAMENT

The earliest documents of the Christian church were written by a mystic: they are the letters of the apostle Paul. St. Paul based his apostolic authority not on having encountered Jesus in the flesh but rather on the road to Damascus. And he seemed to wish that every Christian could have the same interior sense of the love of God "that surpasses knowledge" (Ephesians 3:19).

Technically speaking, Paul's experience on the road to Damascus was more a theophany, a physical manifestation, than a vision, since all three accounts of it in the book of Acts note that others in Paul's traveling party saw a great light or heard a sound, though only he heard the words Jesus spoke (Acts 9:3-8; 22:6-10; 26:12-17). Evelyn Underhill interprets Jesus' words to Paul—"It is hard for you to kick against the goads" (Acts 26:14)—to mean that Paul's spirit was already in turmoil before his experience on the road. Underhill speculates that when Paul saw Stephen stoned and heard him say the heavens opened and he saw Jesus standing at the right hand of God (Acts 7:55-56), Paul may have felt that for all his brutal zeal his faith was missing something glorious and elemental. As Augustine observed, "If Stephen had not prayed, the Church might not have gained Paul."

Apart from his experience on the road to Damascus, Paul also speaks of a mystical ascent into "the third heaven," whether in the body or out of it he did not know, where he heard inexpressible things he is not permitted to tell (2 Corinthians 12:1-10). Paul seems to have broached this topic reluctantly. He speaks of his experience in the third person and moves quickly from his "surpassingly great revelations" (v. 7) to his own weakness. In trying to defend himself against false apostles, Paul brings up financial accountability, his Jewish credentials and his sufferings for Christ before mentioning his ascent into paradise. Some scholars believe that Paul did not dwell on his mystical experience because he knew how easily a craving for signs and wonders can get in the way of one's true life in Christ. As Paul told those same Corinthians, "If I have the gift of prophecy and can fathom all mysteries and all knowledge, and if I have a faith that can move mountains, but have not love, I am nothing" (1 Corinthians 13:2).

Yet Paul did not consider his revelations a kind of spiritual accessory but rather the very foundation of his ministry. He told the Galatians that the gospel he preached was not taught to him by any man; it was received by revelation from Jesus Christ (Galatians 1:1, 11-12). And he asked the Corinthians bluntly, "Am I not an apostle? Have I not seen Jesus our Lord?" (1 Corinthians 9:1). Paul's unshakable confidence in the gospel he had received lent him a sort of fierce tenderness toward those he sought to establish in faith. It also gave him an utter fearlessness, even in the presence of those who held his life in their hands. When he appeared before the magistrates Festus and Agrippa, the latter offered a jaded remark about how Paul seemed to be using a judicial hearing as chance to make some new converts. Paul was not daunted, nor did he disagree: "I pray God that not only you but all who are listening to me today may become what I am, except for these chains" (Acts 26:29).

Where some readers might find Paul's epistles "inspirational" in the generic sense of providing moral uplift, mystical interpreters take his words at face value. For example, when Paul writes, "God's love has been poured into our hearts through the Holy Spirit which has been given to us" (Romans 5:5 RSV), the words, perhaps dulled by overfamiliarity, sound like the kind of rhetorical flourish heard in church services. But for Christian mystics down the ages this is a promise that may be taken quite literally. As Evelyn Underhill puts it, "*Grace,* for Paul, was no theological abstraction, but an actual, inflowing energy, which makes possible man's transition from the natural to the spiritual state." And C. S. Lewis observed that in some of the more baffling passages in Scripture, "God speaks not only for us little ones, but also to great sages and mystics who *experience* what we only *read about* and to whom all the words have therefore different, richer contents."

Though scores of Pauline passages have been incorporated into mystical texts, Bernard McGinn, a leading contemporary authority, identifies 2 Corinthians 3:18 as "one of the most important passages in the history of Christian mysticism." In that verse Paul writes, "And we, who with unveiled faces all reflect the Lord's glory, are being transformed into his likeness with ever-increasing glory, which comes from the Lord, who is the Spirit." McGinn explains that the Greek word translated "reflect" above (*katoptrizein*) also means "contemplate" or even "gaze upon." The verse can be taken to mean that those who contemplate Christ most deeply will come to reflect his nature most fully. As Evelyn Underhill paraphrases this teaching, "He who has seen the Perfect wants to be perfect too."

Lewis interpreted this verse to mean that "a Christian is to Christ as a mirror is to an object." In the same passage he concludes that "in the New Testament the art of life itself is an art of imitation." Spiritual growth as an art of mirroring Christ is one of the most frequently used metaphors in the literature of Christian mysticism. We find the image in the anonymous thirteenth-century "Mirror of Simple Souls" and most especially in John of the Cross and Dante. Lewis singled out *The Paradiso* for its ingenious use of mirror imagery, and he often resorted to such imagery himself. In *The Four Loves,* for example, he notes how hard it is to be truly humble, how we assume our good traits come from some "native luminosity" of our own. He concludes "it is easy to acknowledge, but almost impossible to realise for long that we are mirrors whose brightness, if we are bright, is wholly derived from the sun that shines upon us." Writing in a similar vein in *Mere Christianity,* Lewis says that Christian faith may seem at first to be all about "duties and rules and guilt and virtue." But there are those whose spiritual walk has carried them to a whole other country, where sanctity is not about minding one's morals but about being filled with "goodness as a mirror is filled with light." Lewis adds that these people do not even dwell on "goodness" as such; they are "too busy looking at the source from which it comes."

Apart from Paul, the New Testament writer whom Lewis echoes most often is John, for whom love is also the great theme. Christian mystics quote John's Gospel more than any other, for its prologue about the Word become flesh, and for Jesus' I AM declarations, in which Jesus explains to others that he himself is the gift they are seeking, not secondary benefits such as bread or water or a place of honor in the kingdom.

The book of Revelation, the most extended vision recorded in Scripture, has had less influence on later mystical literature than might be expected. The book's tightly woven symbolism and its apocalyptic message seem less congenial to the mystical mind than other texts that emphasize a sense of joyous participation in the divine life. Revelation, with its new heaven and new earth, provides the framework for the Narnian apocalypse, as recounted in *The Last Battle.* But most of Lewis's borrowings from books attributed to John are less explicit. A typical example comes at the end of *Letters to Malcolm,* where Lewis speculates about the resurrection life, a time when some unfathomed darkness and silence are broken by the dawn of a new day—with birds singing, waters flowing and "the faces of friends [which] laugh upon us with amazed recognition." He is quick to add that this is only a guess, of course. But if not this, then something better: "For we know that we shall be made like Him, for we shall see Him as He is" (1 John 3:2, abridged by Lewis).

EARLY CHRISTIAN MARTYRS

In the first two centuries of the church's life, "laying down one's life for Christ" was seldom seen as simply a metaphor of self-denial. As Lewis observed, "Martyrdom always remains the supreme enacting and perfection of Christianity."

Stephen's mystical vision just before his martyrdom, as recorded in Acts 7, establishes a pattern repeated often during the early centuries of the church's life. No account has survived of the death of Ignatius (c. 35-c. 107), bishop of Antioch, but it is known that he was thrown to wild beasts in the Roman Coliseum during the reign of Emperor Trajan. Shortly before his death Ignatius wrote seven letters to Christian communities under his care, letters that brim with mystical feeling. To the church at Trallia, Ignatius wrote, "I am in chains and able to comprehend heavenly things and the angelic ranks and orderings of principalities, things visible and invisible." But then he quickly adds, "Nevertheless I am not for this reason a disciple," suggesting, like Paul, that transcendent love is greater than transcendent knowledge. To the Romans, Ignatius wrote that he was God's wheat, and once he had been ground by the teeth of wild beasts, he hoped to be found "Christ's pure bread." He asked others not to try to intervene on his behalf, feeling with Paul that to die is gain: "My birth is imminent. Forgive me, brethren; do not prevent me from coming to life."

Another early martyr was Polycarp (c. 69-c. 155), bishop of Smyrna, who may have been appointed to that office by the apostle John. Polycarp was in his eighties when a persecution against Christians broke out in Smyrna, and he took refuge at a farm outside the city. There he saw a vision of his bed engulfed in fire, which he took as a sign that he would be burned at the stake. When he was arrested and brought before the Roman proconsul, Polycarp heard a voice urging him to be of good courage. Urged by Roman officials to deny Christ and swear an oath to Caesar, Polycarp replied, "Eighty-six years have I been his servant and he has done me no wrong. How then can I blaspheme my King who has saved me?" Polycarp was then tied to a stake, praying aloud as the flames rose around him.

It is reported that other martyrs enjoyed a mystical insensibility to pain at the time of their deaths. One Carpus, killed under Emperor Marcus Aurelius (reigned 161-180), laughed after being nailed to a cross. When asked the reason, he explained, "I saw the glory of the Lord and I was glad."

Lewis's friend Charles Williams was particularly moved by the witness of the third-century martyr Felicita, and he recorded her story in *The Descent of the Dove* (1939). In 203 Felicita, eight months pregnant, was arrested in Carthage, North Africa, during the reign of Septimus Severus. She gave birth while in prison awaiting execution, screaming in agony during the delivery. When the guards asked her how she expected to face wild beasts when she could barely endure the pangs of childbirth, she answered: "Now it is I who suffer what I suffer. But then another will suffer with me, because I am to suffer for him." Felicita was taken to the arena with her young friend Perpetua, who also had a small child. The two seemed to steady each other, as Perpetua told of a dream she had had of a golden ladder reaching to heaven, and a voice from above saying calmly, "Welcome, child."

Felicita and Perpetua gave their babies to Christian friends and then entered the arena together. It is said that the wild animals were strangely passive and refused to attack. The noble bearing of the two young women won the sympathy of the crowd, who cried out that they should be spared. Even when soldiers came out under orders and struck them down with swords, Perpetua and Felicita accepted their fate calmly, almost contentedly, as if they knew their names taken together mean "Everlasting Gladness."

CLEMENT AND ORIGEN

Two early church fathers who wrote about mystical elements of their faith were Clement of Alexandria (c. 150-c. 215) and Origen (c. 185-c. 254). Clement, who fled Alexandria during the same persecution in which Felicita and Perpetua were martyred, wrote *Stromateis* ("patchwork"), a loosely ordered collection of essays on faith and knowledge. Clement wrote to explain Christian doctrines to Hellenistic readers, particularly Stoics and Gnostics, trying to show that Christianity was the fulfillment of their own highest religious ideals. Clement was the first to describe what came to be known as the "mystic way," the threefold pattern of purification, illumination and union. Clement defined prayer as "converse with God," something which he felt should be continuous and should permeate a person's whole life.

Origen, also of Alexandria, was one of the first to read the Bible allegorically. His *Commentary on the Song of Songs* interprets that book as an image of the soul in relation to God. Origen calls the purgative (purifying) stage "the winter of the soul" to be followed by a springtime of illumination for those able to put away earthly things. Origen taught that just as the body has five senses, so too does the soul. The soul's inner eye can see visions and its inner ear can hear inaudible voices. It also has a sense of smell to enjoy the "aroma of Christ" (2 Corinthians 2:15), a sense of taste for the "bread of life" and a sense of touch to be able, like John, to grasp the "Word of life" (1 John 1:1). Origen did not use these terms metaphorically or see them as extensions of the imagination. Rather he felt that the soul had its own organs with which to acquire spiritual knowledge. These ideas had tremendous influence on later mystical writers, as did Origen's term "the wound of love" to describe the intense longing of the soul bride for Christ the bridegroom.

Origen is sometimes considered one of the church's earliest heretics because of his interest in the idea of universal salvation. In his treatise *First Principles,* Origen speculated that all evil must eventually yield to the overpowering love of God. He argued that on some final day all fallen humans—and even fallen angels—might surrender their wills to God. Origen went so far as to picture Lucifer himself bowing his head before the Father, the last of all prodigal sons to find his way home.

AUGUSTINE

Augustine of Hippo (354-430) was a bishop in North Africa, a theologian of the first rank and creator of a new genre, the autobiography. He was by far the most influential of the Latin fathers of the church. Augustine was probably a Berber by nationality, the son of a pagan father, Patricius, and a devout Christian mother, Monica. The young Augustine was a brilliant student, and at the age of seventeen he was sent to Carthage to study philosophy and rhetoric. While he was there, Augustine took a mistress who stayed with him thirteen years and bore him a son. For nine years Augustine followed Manichaeism, a dualistic philosophy emphasizing the eternal struggle of light and darkness. Eventually, he became disillusioned with Manichaeism and began studying the Neo-Platonism of Plotinus, a philosophy emphasizing a transcendent, impersonal One from which all things emanate. This One is above both mind (*nous*) and nature (*physis*) and can only be approached through mystical contemplation.

In 383 Augustine traveled to Rome, eventually taking a position as professor of rhetoric in Milan, Italy. At that time the bishop of Milan was Ambrose, whose Christian teachings greatly stirred Augustine's heart. In the incarnation Augustine found a doctrine of God reaching down to redeem the material world, which he had not encountered before in Manichaeism or Neo-Platonism. As he struggled to sort out his beliefs and feelings, Augustine became highly agitated, even to the point of tears. One voice inside him was urging him toward faith: "Be not afraid. He will not withdraw and let you fall. Throw yourself down safely; he will receive and heal you." But another voice asked him if he really thought he could give up all the earthly pleasures he was accustomed to.

The crisis came as he was sitting in a garden and heard the singsong voice of a child saying "Take and read. Take and read." Before him were the epistles of Paul, which he took up and opened at random. There he read Romans 13:13, about behaving decently, avoiding sexual immorality and debauchery. Augustine says he did not need to read any further, for he knew it was time to become a Christian. He told his mother Monica, who had come to live with him in Italy, and was baptized by Ambrose during Easter week in 387.

Later that same year, while they were in Ostia, the port city of Rome, Augustine and his mother were talking about how no earthly delights could compare to the joys of heaven. As they earnestly discussed these matters, they were caught up in a moment of transport vividly described in the *Confessions:*

> Then with our affections burning still more strongly toward the Selfsame [God], we raised ourselves higher and step by step passed over all material things, even the heaven itself from which the sun and moon and stars shine down upon the earth. And still we went upward, meditating and speaking, and looking with wonder at your works, and we came to our own souls, and we went beyond our souls to that region of neverfailing plenty . . . where life is that Wisdom by whom all things are made. . . . And as we talked, yearning towards this Wisdom, we did, with the whole strength of our hearts' impulse, just lightly come into touch with her. And we sighed and left bound there the first fruits of the Spirit, returning to the sounds made by our mouths, where a word has a beginning and an ending.

This famous passage from the *Confessions* is remarkable in several respects. It is the earliest account of the actual stages of mystical transport: from contemplation to a sense of leaving behind the material world to entering the quiet sanctuary of one's own soul to momentarily glimpsing eternal truth. Augustine's description is typical in that the rapturous experience is transitory and it seems to occur in distinct stages. But the account is also highly unusual in that it seems to occur communally, not individually, and that one of those caught up is both uneducated and a woman. In the mystery religions of the ancient world someone like Augustine's mother, however devout, would not be an initiate and would not be considered qualified for mystical experiences.

Monica died soon after the memorable event at Ostia, secure in the knowledge that the son for whom she had prayed for decades had now become a Christian. Four years later Augustine returned to North Africa, where he became a priest and founded a monastic community. In 395 he was consecrated as the bishop of Hippo Regius, and spent the last thirty-five years of his life overseeing the churches in his care, traveling widely and writing over one hundred books and eight hundred sermons. Augustine died in 430, at the age of 76, with Vandals besieging his episcopal city and Christianity falling into eclipse in North Africa.

Though Augustine was called "the Prince of Mystics" by church historian Dom Cuthbert Butler, others have questioned whether he should be considered a mystic at all, since he did not dwell on union with God but only on brief glimpses of eternal Wisdom. Bernard McGinn considers this debate a "dialog of the deaf," essentially a matter of how terms are defined. In a broad survey of Augustine's writings, from classic works such as *Confessions* and *The City of God* to little-known homilies and letters, McGinn concludes that Augustine's ardent Christian faith was indeed rooted in personal experiences of the divine presence in his life. McGinn notes passages like this one in the *Confessions,* in which the bishop, like the psalmist, addresses God directly:

> I entered into my inmost parts with you leading me on. I entered and saw with my soul's eye (such as it was) an unchanging Light above that same soul's eye, above my mind. . . . He who knows truth knows that light, and he who knows it knows eternity. Love knows it. O Eternal Truth and True Love and Beloved Eternity! You are my God, to you I sigh day and night.

Augustine also spoke of "seeing God invisibly" and of enjoying "the presence of the face of God." He was also the first to distinguish between three kinds of visions, a distinction that became standard among later Christian mystics. Augustine believed that sensory visions, things seen with the eyes or heard with the ears, were of the lowest type and could easily be deceptions or illusions. Above these he placed imaginative visions, in which divine truth is communicated through images in the mind's eye or a voice heard within. Highest of all were intellectual visions, truths manifested directly to a person's soul without the mediation of any imagery, from without or within.

Augustine was easily the most influential of the early church fathers, and his influence was certainly not lost on C. S. Lewis. Lewis called him a "great saint and a great thinker to whom my own glad debts are incalculable." Lewis refers to Augustine in a dozen of his books, focusing most often on the Latin father's interpretation of Adam's fall as the sin of pride, and on his definition of evil as the absence of good, not its opposite. Apart from acknowledging Augustine's major contributions as a theologian, Lewis also identified personally with Augustine as an adult convert. (Both became Christians in their early thirties.) Lewis recommended the *Confessions* to new Christians, not only as a spiritual autobiography but also as a rich stimulus for personal devotion and meditation. In *Pilgrim's Regress,* Lewis's spiritual allegory with strong autobiographical overtones, the climactic scene of the young pilgrim's conversion is titled "Securus Te Projice," or "Throw yourself down safely." This is the phrase Augustine reports having heard just before his own plunge into Christian faith.

Lewis seemed to return most often to passages in Augustine that express a sense of spiritual inadequacy, a desire to enlarge one's capacity to experience the fullness of God. In describing his conception of God's glory, Lewis refers to a famous passage in the *Confessions:*

> Late have I loved you, O Beauty, so ancient and so new, late have I
> loved you. You were with me, and I was not with you. . . . Those
> outer beauties kept me far from you, yet if they had not been in you
> they would not have existed at all. You called, you cried out, you
> shattered my deafness: you flashed, you shone, you scattered my
> blindness. . . . You touched me and I burned for your peace.

Lewis also identified with Augustine's plea to God to make his soul a fitting vessel: "The house of my soul is too small for you to come into it. May it be enlarged by you. It is in ruins; restore it."

In Lewis's novel *Till We Have Faces* the protagonist, Queen Orual, recognizes late in life that all her bitter complaints against the gods have been refusals to take responsibility for her own choices. In a moment of epiphany she explains, "I saw well why the gods do not speak to us openly, nor let us answer. . . . Why should they hear the babble that we think we mean? How can they meet us face to face till we have faces?" For readers who know Lewis's devotion to the *Confessions,* it is hard to read this passage without hearing an echo of Augustine's cry of searing self-recognition: "And where was I when I was seeking you? You were there in front of me; but I had gone away—even from myself. I could not find myself, much less find you."

One of the most famous sayings of Augustine, quoted by Lewis in the closing pages of *The Four Loves,* could serve as the epigraph for both men's lives: "Thou hast made us for thyself, and our heart can find no rest till it rests in Thee."

THE "NEGATIVE THEOLOGY" OF GREGORY OF NYSSA AND PSEUDO-DIONYSIUS

Gregory of Nyssa (c. 330-c. 395) was a theologian and bishop of Cappadocia in Asia Minor. Gregory was the first Christian author to describe the spiritual life as a mountain ascent, borrowing the image perhaps from a commentary on Moses by the Jewish philosopher Philo (c. 20 B.C.-c. A.D. 50). Gregory taught that the soul's journey took it from darkness (sin and ignorance) to light (understanding) and back again to darkness (a deeper sense of the ineffable mysteries of God). He believed that the human soul, created in the image of God, was more beautiful than the sun or moon or stars, a mirror "of the Nature that is above every intelligence," a likeness of "the imperishable beauty." Though Gregory emphasized that the fullness of God can never be grasped in this life, he taught that the soul, even in the "darkness" of imperfect faith, was nourished by the sacraments and guided by church teaching, so that it continually ascends toward the summit that awaits beyond the clouded slope.

The sixth-century treatise *Mystical Theology* was long attributed to Dionysius the Areopagite, assumed to be the apostle Paul's disciple mentioned in Acts 17:34. After it was shown that this text was influenced by several early church fathers, especially Gregory of Nyssa, the anonymous author, perhaps a Syrian monk, became known as "Pseudo-Dionysius." Though he wrote three surviving treatises of positive (cataphatic) theology, explaining what can be affirmed about God, Pseudo-Dionysius is best known for his *Mystical Theology,* which strongly emphasizes the incomprehensibility of the Deity, taking the *via negativa* of describing God by what he is not. The prologue of the book, titled "The Divine Dark," sets the tone for the brief, five-chapter treatise:

> O Trinity
> beyond essence and beyond divinity and beyond goodness
> guide of Christians in divine wisdom,
> direct us towards mysticism's heights
> beyond unknowing beyond light beyond limit,
> there where the unmixed and unfettered and unchangeable
> mysteries of theology
> in the dazzling dark of the welcoming silence
> lie hidden, in the intensity of their darkness
> all brilliance outshining, our intellects overwhelming,
> with the intangible and invisible and illimitable:
> Such is my prayer.

Mystical Theology was extremely influential in the Middle Ages, partly because it was thought to come from an associate of Paul and partly because it so eloquently expressed the insufficiency of intellect to plumb the depths of the divine nature. C. S. Lewis discussed Pseudo-Dionysius in *The Discarded Image,* though his interest there was primarily in the other treatises with more positive assertions about the celestial order. But Lewis was keenly aware of the problems posed in trying to make positive assertions about a being who entirely transcends our intellectual grasp. Lewis sounds a bit like Pseudo-Dionysius himself when he argues in *Miracles* that "the burning and undimensioned depth of the Divine Life" is "unconditioned and unimaginable, transcending discursive thought." Yet ultimately Lewis resigns himself to the fact that we must at least resort to metaphors and approximations, lest negative theology collapse into something almost like agnosticism (see chap. seven).

MYSTICISM OF THE MEDIEVAL PERIOD

After several centuries of cultural upheaval from which few records survive, texts produced by Christian mystics began to reemerge in the twelfth century. The dominant figure of that period, both as a mystic and church leader, is Bernard of Clairvaux (1090-1153). Though of noble birth, Bernard took orders as a Cistercian monk in his early twenties, founding a new abbey at Clairvaux, in northeastern France, when he was only twenty-five years old. Bernard was a forceful and charismatic young man, and most of his brothers, an uncle and two dozen other young men joined him at Clairvaux soon after the founding of the new abbey. Despite his frail health Bernard was active in politics all his life, speaking out against persecution of Jews and taking part in all the theological controversies of his day. Though he could be blunt and obstinate in debate, Bernard was considered a visionary and an idealist, and was once called "the conscience of all Europe."

While still a child, Bernard had a dream vision of Mary and the holy child that he remembered all his life. Later his writings would eloquently extol Mary as the mother of God. Bernard also urged his readers to imitate the humility of the Christ child in the manger, "that the great God may not have become a little man without cause."

Bernard is most famous for his sermons on the Song of Songs and his identification of Christ as the Bridegroom or "Word-Spouse." Bernard favored the metaphor of spiritual marriage because it conveyed the idea of union, not as a pantheistic merging of essences but rather as a "communion of wills and an agreement in charity."

Bernard was quite forthright in describing his own mystical experiences, which he described as visits from Christ the Bridegroom:

> So when the Bridegroom, the Word, came to me, he never made known his coming by any signs, not by sight, not by sound, not by touch. . . . Only by the movements of my heart did I perceive his presence. And I knew the power of his might because my faults were put to flight and my human yearnings brought into subjec-

tion. I have marveled at the depth of his wisdom when my secret faults have been revealed and made visible. . . . In the renewal and remaking of the spirit of my mind, that is of my inmost being, I have perceived the excellence of his glorious beauty. And when I contemplate all these things I am filled with awe and wonder at his manifold greatness.

Like most mystics, Bernard stresses the transitory quality of these sublime moments: "O how rare is the hour and how brief its stay." Yet he does not describe mystical ecstasy in terms of high excitation but rather as a state of profound repose: "[The visit to my soul] terrifies not; it soothes; it excites no restless curiosity, but it calms, nor does it fatigue the senses but tranquilizes them. The tranquil God tranquilizes all things, and to behold him is to rest."

Bernard's mystical reveries sometimes took the form of song. One of his most popular hymns, "Jesus, the Very Thought of Thee," is still sung in churches every Sunday, eight centuries after Bernard first offered up these exultant words of praise:

Jesus, the very thought of thee
With sweetness fills my breast;
But sweeter far thy face to see,
And in thy presence rest.

O hope of every contrite heart,
O joy of all the meek,
To those who fall, how kind thou art!
How good to those who seek!

But what to those who find? Ah, this
Nor pen nor tongue can show;
The love of Jesus, what it is,
None but his loved ones know.

Jesus, our only joy be thou,
As thou our prize will be;
Jesus, be thou our glory now,
And through eternity. (Trans. Edward Caswall, 1849)

C. S. Lewis referred to Bernard of Clairvaux as one of the "great spiritual writers" of the Middle Ages. In *Allegory of Love* he cited a French study, *La Théologie Mystique de St. Bernard,* that discusses the widespread influence of Bernard's thought on medieval spirituality and culture. It is most likely that Bernard's celebration of the soul's spiritual marriage with Christ called forth in Lewis's essay "Transposition" the defense of the need to take metaphors from everyday life to describe the nuances of spiritual experience.

Lewis owned a biography of Bernard by Bruno S. James, and it is interesting to note which sentences he underlined. On the one hand he underscored a sentence about Bernard's speaking out against persecution of the Jews. On the other hand Lewis also marked a sentence in the book observing that "one of the many endearing and human traits in the character of Bernard was that he could never see any good in his enemies."

The most well-known saint of the next century after Bernard was Francis of Assisi (1182-1226), also a mystic and also the founder of a new church order. Francis's career is briefly discussed in chapter one (p. 24). In a letter to his friend Arthur Greeves, Lewis called Francis one of the "shining examples of human holiness." Lewis was drawn to Francis's gentle spirit and profound love of nature; he also commended Francis's view of the human body. Unlike Epicureans who would exalt bodily pleasure and comfort above all else, or ascetics who treated their own bodies as vile and unspiritual, Francis simply called his body "Brother Ass," a faithful if lowly and somewhat laughable servant. Lewis enjoyed the metaphor so much that he sometimes whimsically signed his own letters "Bro. Ass."

Francis of Assisi died in 1226, around the same time Thomas Aquinas was born, though the latter was a very different sort of personality. Thomas is famous for his systematizing intellect, best exhibited in his *Summa Theologia,* a treatise that is still considered a doctrinal cornerstone for the teachings of the Roman Catholic Church. As its title suggests, Thomas's monumental work offers a "summary of all theology," combining classical logic with Christian revelation, drawing widely on Aristotle, Augustine, Albertus Magnus and scores of other writers and thinkers. More than seven centuries after it was written, the *Summa* is still considered one of the great intellectual achievements of Western civilization.

Yet Thomas, certainly one of the most scholastic and rationalistic of Christian thinkers, had a mystical side. In 1272, about two years before his death, Thomas had an extraordinary experience during a service of Mass, after which he discontinued work on his still unfinished *Summa.* When urged to return to his life's great project, he answered that what he had seen made everything he had written seem to be made of straw. Thomas never returned to his theological work, and it was completed by his pupil Reginald of Piperno from the outlines and notes Thomas left behind.

Lewis discusses Thomas as a systematic theologian in several scholarly books, referring to him over a dozen times in *The Allegory of Love* and *The Discarded Image* alone. But Lewis also remembered the mysterious episode that occurred near the end of Thomas's life. In *Letters to Malcolm* Lewis observes that the great ideal in prayer is to speak to God as he really is from the depths of ourselves as we really are, without pretensions or evasions. Lewis concludes: "The most blessed result of prayer would be to rise thinking, 'But I never knew before, I never dreamed . . .' I suppose it was at such a moment that Thomas Aquinas said of all his own theology, 'It reminds me of straw.' "

Two of the mystics Lewis read most often and talked about with the greatest warmth and affection were from his own country, the fourteenth-century English writers Walter Hilton and Julian of Norwich. Lewis included both Hilton's *Scale of Perfection* and Julian's *Revelations of Divine Love* on his short list of "great Christian books." He also considered both authors to be more elegant writers than Sir Thomas More, the "man for all seasons" and author of *Utopia* (1516), often praised for his polished prose.

Hilton, the canon of a Midlands priory, is discussed in chapter two (pp. 36-37). Julian (c. 1342-c. 1423) was an anchoress, someone who lived permanently in rooms adjoining a church, at the parish church of St. Julian at Conisford in Norwich. (Julian took her name from the church, so her actual birth name is unknown. Sometimes she is referred to as Lady Julian or Juliana.) As a young woman Julian had prayed she could share in the sufferings of Christ, even to the point of dying at an early age. At the age of thirty she seemed to get her wish, as she fell into a severe illness, losing all feeling in her legs and thought to be near death. As she was receiving last rites, she saw a vision of Christ crucified, followed soon afterward by fifteen more visions. Recovering completely, she wrote a short account of her "showings," as she called them, soon after the experience. Twenty years later she wrote a book recounting each vision and meditating more fully on its doctrinal significance. This longer book, usually called *Sixteen Revelations of Divine Love,* is the first known book written in English by a woman.

The most well known of Julian's visions is one in which Christ places something round, the size of a hazelnut, in her hand. She gazes at the tiny and fragile ball, wondering what it is and marveling that it does not fall to pieces. Then she understands that the frail little bauble in her hand is "all that is made," the entirety of the physical universe. In another vision Christ reassures Julian that despite all indications to the contrary, "All shall be well, all shall be well, all manner of things shall be well." This was a bold and optimistic assertion in fourteenth-century England, the era of the Black Death, the Hundred Years War and the Peasants Revolt. But Julian's visions provided her with a profoundly positive outlook based on her vivid sense of God's nurturing love. Julian felt this quality so strongly that she referred to Christ as "our true Mother" and talked about motherhood as one of the characteristics of the Trinity.

Julian's visions made a deep impression on Lewis, and he refers to her in half a dozen of his books. In a letter written in 1940 to his friend Sister

Penelope, he spends more than a page talking about Julian's vision of holding the whole universe in the palm of her hand and of Christ's reassurances that "All shall be well." He thought it just the right balance to say that the material world is not evil, as the Manichaeans taught, but merely little. He particularly enjoyed the "dream twist" of describing the whole created universe as "so small it might fall to bits." Lewis concluded his sermon "Miracles" with Julian's vision of the hazelnut and referred to it again in *The Four Loves* as a vivid image to help Christians understand how far beneath the majesty of God are even the most magnificent things in his created order. Lewis quoted Julian on Christ's reassurance that "All shall be well" in *The Great Divorce, The Problem of Pain* and again in his essay "Psalms," collected in *Christian Reflections*. Clearly, Julian is the sort of person Lewis had in mind when he described mysticism (in the same paragraph where he discusses the hazelnut vision) as "wonderful foretastes of the fruition of God vouchsafed to some in their earthly life."

Another fourteenth-century text Lewis knew well and recommended for meditative reading is the *Theologia Germanica,* or "German Theology." Written by someone identified simply as a "man from Frankfurt," the *Theologia* teaches that the great drama of life is the struggle between God's will and self-will, between what it calls "Godhood" and "I-hood." God is, by his very nature, self-giving, self-emptying, even to the point of descending into human flesh and dying on a cross. Humans by nature are just the opposite; we are almost literally "full of ourselves." We think that happiness lies in expanding the realm of our I-hood, argues the *Theologia,* when it actually lies in the exact opposite direction, partaking more and more of the divine nature, and being freed from our own selfish natures. This process is "the mystical way," a deliberate regimen of purgation, illumination and eventual soul-communion with God.

The *Theologia* frequently treats heaven and hell as states of the soul long before they become places of eternal reward or punishment. According to this text the devil cast himself out of heaven when he began claiming things for himself in a greedy spirit of "I, and me and mine." Adam made the same mistake in the Garden, grasping the forbidden fruit with that same possessive, self-willed spirit of "I, me and mine." For the *Theologia,* the love of money is only one expression of a deeper root of all evil: "Hell is nothing but self-will; if there were no self-will, there would be no devil and no hell."

The *Theologia* was especially influential in the German Reformation. Martin Luther said that after the Bible and the writings of Augustine this text is the one that most influenced his thinking. Lewis too acknowledged his debts to the *Theologia.* In discussing the proper relation between Christianity and secular learning, Lewis cites the *Theologia* as one of his Christian authorities, along with the New Testament, Augustine, Thomas Aquinas, John Milton and John Henry Newman. In *The Problem of Pain* Lewis quotes twice from the *Theologia,* once on the natural self's horror at submitting to a life in Christ and once on loving God simply for his goodness, not out of longing for rewards or fear of punishment.

POST-REFORMATION MYSTICS

It is generally acknowledged that the Protestant Reformation of the sixteenth century brought about a decline in Christian mysticism, both because of its rejection of monastic institutions and also its emphasis on a more fully rationalized theology. Though Lewis grew up in the north of Ireland, where the relations between Catholics and Protestants have generally been strained, he was determined after his conversion to be a "mere Christian," someone who sought to learn from all those respected for their mature faith. Thus, in Lewis's books and letters, he refers to and recommends texts by Roman Catholic mystics such as Teresa of Ávila, Brother Lawrence and Blaise Pascal along with those by the Protestant authors that a devout Anglican would be expected to read. Two mystics of the Catholic Reformation (the Counter-Reformation) whom he seems to have benefited from the most were the Spaniard John of the Cross and the French abbot Francis de Sales.

John of the Cross was born as Juan de Yepes near Ávila, Spain. Though his parents were too poor to send him to school, his intellectual gifts and spiritual earnestness were evident even in childhood, and a well-to-do local patron paid for his education at Jesuit schools and his university training at Salamanca. John took the name John of the Cross at the time of his ordination in 1567, and soon afterward he met Teresa of Ávila, an encounter that changed the course of his life.

Teresa, then fifty-two, had taken holy orders as a young woman but did not emerge as a mystical personality until she was in her forties, when she began reporting visions, locutions and even experiences of bodily levitation. In 1562 Teresa was given permission to establish a new order of reformed Carmelite nuns. The Carmelites had originated in the twelfth century as an order of hermits living at the foot of Mount Carmel in Palestine, where Elijah had called down fire on his altar to the Lord. By Teresa's time the Carmelites had become relaxed in their spiritual disciplines and indulgent in their style of living. She established the reformed order, called the Discalced (Barefoot) Carmelites, to return to the simplicity and spiritual rigor of the original order. Teresa founded houses for her new order all over Spain, often against great opposition from the more worldly Carmelites.

When Teresa met John of the Cross, they agreed he should begin a similar reformed Carmelite order for men. When he began to undertake this project, however, opposition was so fierce John was actually kidnapped and held captive for eight months. While imprisoned, John was flogged, starved and denied the sacraments. This experience left John feeling he had been utterly stripped of everything except his faith in God. He wrote mystical poetry on scraps of paper in his cramped cell (the broom closet of a monastery), which formed the basis of his later mystical treatises after he escaped his captors and resumed his position as spiritual director in one of the reformed Carmelite houses.

Apart from his poetry, still considered some of the finest written in Spanish, John of the Cross is now best known for his two-part treatise *The Ascent of Mount Carmel* and *The Dark Night of the Soul*. In these two books John offers a detailed exploration of the spiritual itinerary of purgation, illumination and union. His writing is often poetic and paradoxical, a return to the tradition of via negativa of Gregory of Nyssa and

Pseudo-Dionysius (whose writings John had studied). For example, John offered this advice to new pilgrims just beginning their journey up Mount Carmel:

> To enjoy what you have not
> You must go by a way you enjoy not;
> To find the knowledge you have not
> You must go by a way you know not;
> To become what you are not
> You must go by a way in which you are not.

John of the Cross is most often associated with the phrase "the dark night of the soul," but this topic is only a small part of his teaching. And the phrase itself is often misunderstood, as if it were merely a poetic way to describe despair. The sixteenth-century Spanish word *escura* can be rendered as either "dark" or "obscure," and John's phrase contains something of both meanings. He envisions the first part of the dark night as a kind of twilight, a leaving behind of worldly comforts and se-curities. Then comes the "darkness" of exploring the mysteries of the di-vine nature, as if traveling by starlight. The final stage of the dark night, which John sees as only for the most spiritually adept, is an utter relin-quishing of self, a painful death of the ego that leads to an eventual dawn, a whole level of illumination in the seeker's understanding of God and his purposes.

In his essay "The Psalms" in *Christian Reflections,* Lewis contrasts the true dark night of the soul, an experience only for those at a "higher level" of spiritual understanding, with something much more com-mon—a "dark night of the flesh." Lewis coined this phrase to describe the emotional state of someone who has become a byword and a pariah, someone who internalizes the scorn of others and who seems to mix self-loathing with loathing for others. While the true dark night of the soul is a purifying experience, Lewis describes the dark night of the flesh as a neurosis to be overcome, a truly destitute spiritual condition.

In *Letters to Malcolm* Lewis wonders how the mystical experience of a

Christian like John of the Cross would differ from that of a pre-Christian mystic like Plotinus. This is the passage in which Lewis declares that we take the mysticism of saints seriously because of their saintliness; we do not declare them saintly because they report having mystical experiences. In the same book Lewis shows that he understands John aright when he states, "It is saints, not common people, who experience the 'dark night.' " Lewis notes the paradox that it is sometimes those who are nearest to God who feel most painfully his "hiddenness." He goes on to speculate that the greatest of all dark nights was the one experienced by Christ on the cross, in his sense of utter abandonment by the Father.

Another Catholic Reformation mystic from whom Lewis seemed to draw a great deal of spiritual sustenance was Francis de Sales (1567-1622). Francis was the son of a nobleman, born at the Castle de Sales in Savoy, a province in France near Geneva. The Calvinist revolution in Geneva in the late sixteenth century affected that whole region of Europe, and Francis, as a young man, seriously considered converting to the new creed. But in his early twenties he underwent a profound depression that lasted several weeks, a feeling that he was not among the elect, abandoned by God. While tearfully kneeling in prayer at a church in Paris, Francis heard a voice in his heart say, "I do not call myself the Damning One. I am Jesus." Francis felt a great burden fall away and he arose certain that God, in his abundant grace, offered love and salvation to all who sought it. This experience left a lifelong imprint on Francis's personality. There was a spirit of gentleness and compassion in both his personal demeanor and in his writings.

Though his father wished him to study law and become a magistrate, Francis took holy orders instead and soon gained a reputation as an eloquent preacher, caring pastor and effective spiritual director. At the relatively young age of thirty-five he was appointed bishop of Geneva in 1602. Since his episcopal city at that time was controlled by the Calvinists, however, Francis's work actually centered in Annecy, in his native province of Savoy. Besides engaging in frequent debates with Calvinists, Francis also composed two devotional classics, *Introduction to a Devout*

Life (1602) and *Treatise on the Love of God* (1616). The first of these books is mainly a practical guide to spiritual growth for those who live in the world, not the cloister. The second book is the more mystical of the two, depicting the soul's communion with God in a series of striking metaphors: ivy climbing a great tree, a child nursed by its mother, a honeybee attracted by the color and fragrance of a blossom. Francis describes his own mystical experiences in the *Treatise,* saying there is something greater than the sense of rapture a person may experience in times of deep prayer. This purer ecstasy may be found by one whose entire life is "elevated and united to God" through forsaking worldly desires and his or her natural will, inclining instead to "interior gentleness, simplicity, humility, and above all charity."

Lewis wrote that even in the years when he despised Christianity, he couldn't help but recognize a certain "honey-eyed and floral" quality in the writings of Francis de Sales. He later added that Francis is one of those writers who shows you the "beauty of holiness." Lewis also recommended a chapter in *Introduction to a Devout Life* called "Of Meekness Towards Ourselves," where Francis tells his readers that self-denial should not lead to self-hatred, that a Christian should recognize personal mistakes "with mild and calm remonstrances." Citing also Julian of Norwich's advice that an individual should be "loving and peaceable" not only to other Christians but also to oneself, Lewis concludes that true Christian renunciation lies in self-forgetfulness instead of self-contempt. In *Letters to Malcolm* Lewis again commended the gentle spirit of Francis, contrasting the Puritan teaching about seeing the self as an utterly unworthy toad to Francis's "green, dewy chapter on *la douceur* ("softness") towards one's self."

In general, Lewis expresses respect and admiration for a wide range of contemplative writers, even those disciplinarians like Ignatius Loyola and William Law, whom he finds "stringent." But his real warmth and affection seems most evident when he is discussing the more softhearted mystics such as Julian of Norwich, Walter Hilton, Francis de Sales and George MacDonald.

～ ～ ～

Apart from the figures discussed above, we also find references in Lewis's books and letters to Nicholas of Cusa, Thomas à Kempis, Ignatius Loyola, *The Cloud of Unknowing* as well as twentieth-century mystics such as Simone Weil and Sundar Singh (discussed on p. 104). It is also interesting to note that among Lewis's most beloved poets were those with strong mystical overtones—Dante, George Herbert, Henry Vaughan, William Wordsworth and George MacDonald.

Considering his lifelong interest in mystical texts, it is not surprising that Lewis himself should appear in an anthology called *The Protestant Mystics* (1964), introduced by the distinguished poet W. H. Auden. (The collection includes excerpts from *Surprised by Joy* as examples of numinous longing, or *Sehnsucht*.) Though he did not use the term as a self-designation, it seems fitting that someone whose own reading and writing so often manifests his fascination with experiences of the "Mighty Beauty" should himself come to be known as one of the mystics of Christian tradition.

~ *Four* ~

THE MYSTICAL WAY
IN THE SPACE TRILOGY

*I*n *The Problem of Pain* C. S. Lewis suggests the first humans might also be considered the first mystics. He pictures Adam and Eve in their unfallen state as creatures who have direct communication with their Creator and who enjoy a perfect union of their wills with his. Lewis assumes the first humans were also blessed with a harmony of mind, soul and spirit beyond what any Hindu mystic might claim.

But with the first act of disobedience, the first assertion of the self over its Source, came not only estrangement from God but also inner divisions of mind and body, of reason and passion, of the higher faculties with the lower appetites. Lewis concludes we are all "in Adam": we are a "spoiled species" who must learn through the hard lesson of obedience how to "tread Adam's dance backwards," to submit our wills in order to heal our inner discords and "retrace our long journey from Paradise."

Of course, this journey to the soul's true home begins at the moment of repentance, when a person accepts Christ. But theologians typically distinguish between *justification,* the moment of redemption through Christ's atoning work, and *sanctification,* the lifelong process of "putting on Christ," growing in spiritual wholeness.

For many, the process of sanctification means believing in Christ and

* PROTESTANT THEOLOGIANS ONLY?

obeying his commandments. But from the earliest era of the church there have been those who have espoused the *mystica theologia,* "mystical theology," a belief that Christians should strive to experience the presence of God directly in their lives. This goes beyond the ordinary faculties of intellect, will, imagination and feelings. It is a reaching out beyond the limits of ordinary consciousness, a disciplined program for developing one's spiritual intuitions in order to see with the eyes of the soul, to attend fully to the "still small voice" within.

As noted in chapter three, it was the second-century church father Clement of Alexandria who first described what came to be known as the "mystic way," a threefold process of purgation, illumination and union. Purgation means "purification," setting aside the elements of selfishness and worldliness that keep us fettered to the here and now. Illumination is an enlargement of spiritual understanding beyond the reach of ordinary reason. Union is a state of rest in which one's will is continuously at unity with God's will.

The term *union,* in this context, should not be confused with the pantheistic idea that the human and divine are ultimately one. The twelfth-century mystic philosopher Meister Eckhart stressed his goal of union with God so emphatically that he spent the last years of his life battling charges of heresy. Teresa of Ávila also faced inquiries by church officials, until she made it clear that by *union* she did not mean sharing the divine essence but rather a habitual, almost effortless "walking with God." For Eastern Orthodox mystics such as Gregory of Palamas (c. 1296-1359), believers may be united with "divine energies," but not with the unknowable "divine essence." Because the word *union* can be so easily misunderstood, mysticism scholar Georgia Harkness prefers the term *communion.* The leading contemporary authority on mysticism, Bernard McGinn, also avoids the word *union,* preferring to speak instead of mystics learning to live in the *presence* of God.

C. S. Lewis was familiar with the mystic way—the threefold path of purgation, illumination and union—from his reading of medieval theology, especially texts such as the *Theologia Germanica* and *The*

Scale of Perfection. The mystic way was also engagingly explained for modern readers by Evelyn Underhill, whose classic books such as *Mysticism, The Mystic Way* and *Mystics of the Church* were much admired by Lewis.

This admiration turned out to be mutual. Soon after the first book of Lewis's Space trilogy, *Out of the Silent Planet,* was published in 1938, he received a glowing letter from Underhill, which he later acknowledged as "one of the high lights of my literary life." Lewis replied to her letter that as a relatively new Christian he was frankly overwhelmed to be noticed and praised by someone of her stature.

Lewis must have been especially pleased to have the first book of the Space trilogy honored by the leading British scholar on mysticism. For these three books, *Out of the Silent Planet* (1938), *Perelandra* (1943) and *That Hideous Strength* (1945), provide Lewis's imaginative embodiment of the mystic way in a modern context.

It may seem odd to read interplanetary adventure stories as tales of a mystical journey. But in writing about fantasy novels Lewis explained what he thought " 'other planets' are really good for in fiction." He commented that "no merely physical strangeness or merely spatial distance will realize the idea of otherness which is what we are always trying to grasp in a story about voyaging through space: you must go into another dimension. To construct plausible and moving 'other worlds' you must draw on the only real 'other world' we know, that of the spirit."

For Lewis the "other-world of the spirit" suggested not only imagination but a real Otherworld, things not seen but affirmed by faith. So it was only natural for someone with his teeming imagination and keen convictions to write stories in which a cosmic voyage becomes also a spiritual pilgrimage.

AN OUTLINE OF THE MYSTIC WAY

In her classic study of the mystic way, Evelyn Underhill found the traditional formula—purgation, illumination, union—a bit too broad. Having read widely in Christian mysticism from the second century

to the twentieth, she found it more useful to describe not three stages
but five:

1. *The awakening of the self to divine reality.* A sudden new awareness
of the Supreme Splendor, usually accompanied by peace and exultation, which may be experienced even by those who are already reli-
giously devout.

2. *Purgation.* A consciousness of the self's finiteness and imperfection,
its many illusions and its distance from God. A disciplined effort to
cleanse the impurities that dim spiritual awareness.

3. *Illumination.* An inner journey of many stages (including detours
and setbacks) that enlarges one's understanding of the Absolute, and
pries the self away from worldly desires and petty concerns. (Underhill
stresses that purgation and illumination seldom occur as distinct stages.
Rather they alternate between pain and pleasure, between grievous de-
nials of the self and joyous moments of liberation.)

4. *The dark night of the soul.* Sometimes called the "mystic death" or
"spiritual crucifixion," this is the culmination of the purification-illumina-
tion process, one which many "pilgrims of the inner odyssey" never reach.
This is the surrender of "the very center of I-hood, the will," an agonizing
death of self, often accompanied by a sense of God's absence, a desolation
in the inner being just when one feels most in need of reassurance.

5. *Union.* The final goal of the mystic quest, a revival from "mystic
death" in which the soul no longer struggles, no longer oscillates between pains of denial and pleasures of discovery. It is a state of equilibrium, of "peaceful joy, enhanced powers, and intense certitude." Contemplatives often refer to this as the soul's mystical marriage with God.

Lewis's Space trilogy illustrates Underhill's summary of the mystic
way, both in its broad outline and in particular details. At the beginning
of the trilogy its central character, Elwin Ransom, is a good but timid
man, someone not at all inclined to adventure. But by the time he has
voyaged to Mars and Venus, and foiled a diabolical plot here on earth,
Ransom has become another man entirely: a peer of prophets, friend of
angels, scion of Arthurian kings.

OUT OF THE SILENT PLANET

In the first paragraph of *Out of the Silent Planet* the protagonist is not introduced by name but rather referred to as "the Pedestrian." The term seems appropriate enough to describe a man on a walking tour, waiting out a thundershower under a chestnut tree. But the word is capitalized all three times it is used, as if referring to an allegorical pilgrim out of John Bunyan, one whose outer journey will reflect his soul's progress.

In the second paragraph the Pedestrian is identified as Ransom, a Cambridge philologist on a solitary walking tour. He is a tall, round-shouldered man, thirty-five to forty, with a certain shabbiness of dress that marks a university professor on holiday. At first glance we cannot help but notice how much this description fits Lewis himself. He was in his late thirties when he wrote *Out of the Silent Planet*. He was of middle height and was described as round-shouldered by more than one who knew him. And his shabbiness of dress was legendary. Those who first met him often thought he looked more like a gardener, a butcher or a country farmer than a university don. Continuing in *Out of the Silent Planet* readers soon learn that Ransom is a bachelor, an antivivisectionist and a Christian. All of these traits remind us again of the author himself. Lewis commented that Ransom was not meant to be a self-portrait. But whatever his intentions, he created in Ransom a character whose convictions and consciousness closely resembled his own.

The opening pages of *Out of the Silent Planet* describe experiences that Lewis himself might have had on one of his walking tours. But when Ransom stops in at an isolated country house being rented by Edward Weston, a noted scientist, and Dick Devine, a former schoolmate, his adventures begin in earnest. Sensing something vaguely sinister about their intentions toward a simpleminded boy who works for them, Ransom nevertheless accepts a drink, discovering too late that he has been drugged. He loses consciousness and dreams about trying to escape from a walled garden, getting stuck with one leg outside the wall and one leg inside.

This dream marks Ransom's departure from the world of the ordinary and his entry into other worlds. The contents of the dream make little sense to someone reading *Out of the Silent Planet* for the first time, but later readings reveal it to be a symbolic prophecy of Ransom's adventures on Mars and Venus. The garden represents planet Earth, and Ransom's straddling position suggests that from this time forth he will have a dual identity—partly a dweller of this world, partly a citizen of other worlds.

When he starts to come to, Ransom makes a feeble attempt to escape, but he is soon knocked unconscious again. Awakening the next time in an eerie metal chamber, he realizes he is traveling in space and feels poised between "delirious terror or an ecstasy of joy." He fears for his own sanity as he contemplates the idea of traveling so far from earth into the dark vastness that separates the worlds. But when he looks out the window, Ransom is not appalled but rather awed by the splendid scene spread before his eyes. He sees "planets of unbelievable majesty, and constellations undreamed of," which look like "celestial sapphires, rubies, emeralds and pin-pricks of burning gold" sparkling upon the fabric of "undimensioned, enigmatic blackness."

As the voyage continues Ransom feels there must be a "spiritual cause for his progressive lightening and exultation of heart." He comes to realize that the modern concept of space, suggesting a vast, cold, dead abyss between the planets, seems an almost blasphemous term to describe the "empyrean ocean of radiance in which they swam." Ransom concludes that "older thinkers had been wiser when they named it simply the heavens—the heavens which declared the glory," thus choosing the words of the psalmist (Psalm 19:1) over those of the scientist.

In her laudatory letter to Lewis, Evelyn Underhill singled out this episode for particular praise. Underhill seemed to take special delight in Ransom's sudden epiphany, his radical change of perception whereby his terror of dark, empty space is turned to rapture at the glad radiance of "the Heavens."

Underhill may have enjoyed this passage in particular because it illustrates so well what she called "the soul's awakening." In her seminal study *Mysticism,* Underhill notes that many a mystical journey has begun with a ravishing, transformative experience of nature. She explains that, often abruptly and unexpectedly, the world may become saturated with significance:

> In these hours the world seems charged with a new vitality, with a splendour which does not belong to it but is poured through it, as light through a coloured window, grace through a sacrament. . . . In such moods of heightened consciousness, each blade of grass seems fierce with meaning and becomes a well of wondrous light: a little emerald set in the City of God.

Having awakened to a whole new set of realities, Ransom begins a long pilgrimage of alternating purgations and illuminations. Lewis called *Out of the Silent Planet* "Ransom's *enfance,*" portraying Ransom as a man who, though in his middle years, is in his soul's childhood.

Indeed, on the voyage to Mars, Ransom is compared to a "frightened child." Overcoming fear is the first great task Ransom faces. Though he is a Cambridge don, a distinguished linguist and a religious man, his attainments and beliefs are not a very present help in time of trouble. Critic Chad Walsh has correctly noted that Ransom's "one besetting sin is anxiety."

On the voyage to Mars, Ransom indeed has excellent reasons to be afraid. He has been drugged, knocked over the head, kidnapped, dragged into outer space and has overheard a conversation about his being turned over to some alien beings called sorns. This last bit of news plays havoc with his already overcharged imagination. Having (like Lewis) grown up reading science fiction, Ransom visualizes aliens with "twitching feelers, rasping wings, slimy coils, and curling tentacles," assuming they will embody some "monstrous union of superhuman intelligence and insatiable cruelty."

Once Ransom and his abductors land on Mars, his first surprise is to find a landscape of surpassing beauty. Later on, he will learn that the inhabitants of Mars, who call their world Malacandra, are not at all like the nightmarish visions of his imagination. There are three rational species on the planet, very different from each other but all benign and living in harmony. Escaping from Weston and Devine, Ransom wanders on his own for a while and then befriends human-sized otterlike creatures called hrossa, learning some of their speech. A pious man, he begins to wonder if he should undertake to instruct them in his faith. But they have their own well-defined convictions, and it is they who marvel at his ignorance. They tell him that their world is ruled by Oyarsa, who is himself subject to Maleldil the Young, who created their world and who lives with the Old One.

After further conversations with another rational species, the sorns, and with Oyarsa, the ruler of Malacandra, Ransom comes to understand that Maleldil the Young created the Field of Arbol (the solar system) and all the beings in it. He chose an Oyarsa, or tutelary intelligence, to rule each world, served by nearly imperceptible beings called eldila. However, on the third planet the Oyarsa and some of his eldils rose up in rebellion against Maleldil, recognizing no authority but themselves. Led by the "Bent Oyarsa," this world was now cut off from the others and thus called Thulcandra, "the Silent Planet." It remains a battleground, though there are rumors in "Deep Heaven" of wondrous things performed by Maleldil to reclaim his lost world.

This is certainly the stuff of science fiction. It is also orthodox Christian theology, as it might be understood in an unfallen, hierarchical world. In response to inquiries about the trilogy's symbolism Lewis explained straightforwardly that the Old One and Maleldil the Young represent the Father and the Son of the Trinity, that eldils represent angels, and the Bent One is Satan. Lest it seem blasphemous to add new chapters to Christian doctrine, he also explained that his stories were a form of "imagining out loud," speculations in fiction about "what God might be supposed to have done in other worlds."

For Ransom it is a revelation to discover that what he thought of as his "religion" is simply reality. In his voyages to other worlds the distinction between natural and supernatural is completely erased. This truth is brought home even more fully when he begins to experience directly that which he has formerly only believed in—angels (called eldils in the trilogy).

At first Ransom is completely unaware of the presence of eldils on Malacandra. The first time Ransom comes near an eldil, he does not see it at all. The next one he meets can hardly be distinguished from "imagination and the dance of sunlight on the lake." Ransom's hrossan host explains that eldila are difficult to see because light passes through them, and they don't always wish to be seen. But as Ransom becomes accustomed to life on Malacandra, he begins to notice what he calls "footsteps of light" and to hear "silvery noises in the air."

When asked about his portrayal of eldils as nearly invisible, Lewis replied that he was drawing on the medieval idea that angels have bodies made of ether, the lighter-than-air substance which fills the space between heavenly spheres. But Lewis also noted, referring to *Out of the Silent Planet,* that "any amount of theology can be smuggled into people's minds under cover of romance without their knowing it." This suggests his portrayal of the eldils was part of a larger strategy to help readers look at old doctrines with new eyes. If eldils appeared to Ransom clad in radiant garments and announced, "Fear not," their identity would be so recognizable as to be dismissible. Lewis enjoyed subverting his readers' certainty about the barriers between the natural and the supernatural, between myth and history. Indeed, after reading all three books of the trilogy, readers may find themselves giving every peculiar slant of light a second look, thinking perhaps, *Why it's only the moonlight filtering through the trees—and yet for a moment . . .*

Though Ransom meets angels in *Out of the Silent Planet* and even consults with Oyarsa, the archangel who rules the planet, he does not encounter God (Maleldil) directly. But Malacandra has its own mystics. When Ransom asks his hrossan friend Hyoi if the fear of death casts a pall over what seems like an otherwise perfect world, Hyoi answers by recounting what he calls "a day in my life that has shaped me."

Hyoi goes on to explain that when he was very young, he climbed up to the Martian highlands "where the stars shine at midday" to a great waterfall called the Mountain of Water. Hyoi calls this "the place of most awe in all worlds" and says that there he was alone with Maleldil, and that ever since then "my heart has been higher, my song deeper." He concludes that he drank of life that day, the best drink he would ever have except for one—"Death itself in the day I drink it and go to Maleldil." Translated into more familiar terms, Hyoi's words echo those of Paul: "For to me, to live is Christ and to die is gain" (Philippians 1:21).

Despite the reassurances of Hyoi and others of his kind, Ransom's anxiety about meeting some alien monstrosity on this planet reemerges when he first travels to meet a sorn, and later when he is called for an audience with Oyarsa. Yet as the story progresses, we can see that his nearly debilitating fears early in his adventure are becoming more and more manageable. When Ransom does eventually meet a large insectlike creature called a pfifltrigg, he finds it comic rather than horrific. (The name pfifltrigg is, in fact, Lewis's coinage, from two Old Icelandic words combined to mean "safe monster.")

At the end of *Out of the Silent Planet* Ransom serves as translator so that Weston and Devine can try to explain themselves to Oyarsa (whom they cannot see and dismiss as a deception of some kind). Oyarsa discovers how truly depraved these fallen humans are, the one by ruthless self-love, the other by a ruthless ideology of human conquest over other worlds. In the end, the ruler of that world determines that all three should return to where they came from.

Before returning to his home planet, which will never again quite be home, Ransom receives this farewell counsel from the presiding spirit of Malacandra: "You are guilty of no evil, Ransom of Thulcandra, except a little fearfulness. For that, the journey you go on is your pain, and perhaps your cure: for you must be either mad or brave before it is ended." The return flight is indeed a difficult one, and Ransom does emerge largely purged of his fears. But most of his cure came on Malacandra itself. One can see how different a person Ransom has become by comparing his terror at watching the "Earthrise" from space early in the story (pp. 22-24) to his exultant memories of watching the planet Jupiter rise from Malacandra in the closing pages of the book (pp. 159-60).

PERELANDRA

By the end of *Out of the Silent Planet* the pilgrim has indeed made a great deal of progress. But Ransom's journey of purification and illumination is far from over, as can be seen in the next novel of the trilogy, *Perelandra*. If the great challenge of Ransom's first journey was to overcome his fears, the great challenge of his second journey is to overcome his self-will.

Though Ransom was taken to Mars against his wishes, he voluntarily accepts a mission to Venus, traveling naked in a translucent coffin-shaped box and carried through the heavens by the hand of an eldil. If Ransom found Malacandra to be surprisingly beautiful when he first arrived there, he is positively ravished with pleasure on plummeting into the ocean of the second planet, called Perelandra. With warm sweet-water seas surrounding him and a golden dome of sky above, Ransom finds that even an accidental mouthful of water from a passing wave gives him "quite astonishing pleasure almost like meeting Pleasure itself for the first time." Even the violent squall that rises up leaves him more dazzled than frightened. The thunder is more resonant than terrestrial thunder, making a kind of tinkling sound in the distance, "the laugh, rather than the roar, of heaven."

Like Malacandra, with its utopian society of divergent species all living in peace, Perelandra too is an unfallen planet. It is an Edenic world of golden seas and lush tropical islands that float upon the waves. Besides these delights, Perelandra also evokes a whole other species of pleasure. When Ransom, riding on a dolphin's back at night, approaches one of the floating islands, he experiences a sense of rapture somehow strangely familiar, a "cord of longing," which seems to have been fastened before he ever came to Perelandra, before his earliest childhood, before even the foundations of the world. For Ransom this yearning, with both its pain and pleasure, seems "sharp, sweet, wild, and holy, all in one."

In this passage we see Perelandra, not only as a garden of unearthly delights but as an image of Joy itself. The exotic garden—whether Eden, Hesperides or Avalon—is one of the places that Lewis associated with

SEE p. 92

Joy from early childhood on. The luxuriant islands, too, appear throughout Lewis's books, most notably in *Pilgrim's Regress,* as a picture of unreachable paradise.

But Ransom has not come to Perelandra for his own pleasure. He has
been sent on a mission not yet revealed to him. This quest does not begin
on a promising note, however: the Green Lady, the Eve of Perelandra,
bursts into laughter at Ransom's appearance the first time she sees him.
On the voyage to Venus in a translucent casket, one side of his body has
been burned brownish red by the sun and the other left a pallid white.
She apologizes for her first reaction, but nonetheless she dubs him "Piebald Man," not a very dignified sobriquet for a man sent to save a planet.

Ransom's two-toned body is an image of his divided self. Though he
has submitted to the will of Maleldil (God), he still has within him his
natural self, his own desire for control, safety and self-reliance. Ransom's
piebald state recalls his dream in *Out of the Silent Planet,* in which he
found himself straddling a garden wall—half a citizen of a fallen world,
half a citizen of Deep Heaven.

Critics have applied a variety of psychological models to explain Ransom's dual nature. But Ransom's inner discord here can best be understood in terms of the traditional Christian paradigms, the conflict between what the *Theologia Germanica* calls "God-hood" and "I-hood."

In *Out of the Silent Planet* Ransom learned a great deal about goodness,
especially about diverse creatures living in harmony and how they accepted change and mortality as inevitable parts of the life process. In *Perelandra* he is forced to confront the nature of evil. As he considers its origins, he comes to realize it is not only "out there," in rebel angels or
demented visionaries like Weston; it is also "in here," latent within himself and even in the unfallen Eve of another world. He comes to realize
that evil may come into a perfect world not because there are positive
evils attempting to seduce him but because he is tempted to cling to
good things desired over good things given.

This truth unfolds itself gradually in Ransom's mind. Not long after
arriving on the planet, he tastes the nectar from a yellow fruit and finds

it inexpressibly delicious, a whole new kind of pleasure that on earth would lead to wars and the conquest of nations. He finds in this spectacular new delight something deserving of "an oratorio or a mystical meditation." But as he goes to take a second drink, a vague instinct within tells him not to, that partaking again would be an excess, like demanding to hear the same symphony twice in one day.

The next day Ransom finds another exquisite delight when he touches the bubble from a Perelandran bubble tree and it bursts in his face. He feels the urge to plunge through the whole lot of bubbles to multiply the enchantment tenfold, but again he is restrained by some inner adviser. This time, though, he is able to identify the source of his restraint. He sees that this "itch to have things over again" is the source of much evil, that one's life is not a roll of film that can be unrolled twice. He wonders if the love of money is called the root of all evil because wealth provides "a defence against chance, a security for being able to have things over again." This lesson, learned from a fruit tree and a bubble tree, becomes one of the predominant themes of *Perelandra*. Humans long for a godlike sovereignty over their lives, to maximize pleasure and security, to wall out pain and uncertainty. But only when they learn to accept vicissitudes and vulnerability as inherent to the fabric of life can they truly be free. *IN AN "UNFALLEN" world?*

When Ransom later explains the nature of evil to the Green Lady, the Eve of that world, he amplifies this theme. Though she inhabits a world where everything is good, she herself could become the instrument by which evil enters in. Ransom reminds her that when she first saw him from afar, she thought he was her husband, the Adam of that planet, from whom she had become separated. She had been disconcerted for a moment—only a moment—and then adjusted to the new circumstance. But, Ransom asks, what if she had clung to her old expectation, refusing to exchange her hope to find her husband for the novel experience of meeting someone from another world? The Green Lady comprehends this, thinking of times she had gone looking for one kind of fruit and found another. She says that we would make the fruit we found taste insipid by continuing to long for the one we expected.

The Green Lady's recognition of how evil might enter into her heart applies at the cosmic level as well. Building on her understanding about taking the good that comes instead of clinging to the good expected, Ransom identifies the Bent One as an eldil who "clung longer—who has been clinging since before the worlds were made." The Green Lady responds that the old good would cease to be good if one did that, and Ransom agrees: "Yes. It has ceased. And still he clings." The Bent One (Lucifer) was granted one of the greatest of all goods—to be Maleldil's viceroy over a world. Yet he would accept no sovereign over him, considering equality with Maleldil as a thing to be grasped. And the temptation to which he fell becomes the one he will tempt humans with: "You shall be as gods."

In Genesis the one thing forbidden to Adam and Eve was to taste fruit of the tree of knowledge of good and evil, to try to achieve a godlike omniscience on their own. On Perelandra the forbidden thing is to dwell on the "Fixed Land," the one continent on their world that does not float upon its golden seas. Maleldil has decreed the floating islands to be the proper home of the king and queen of Perelandra, and he has forbidden them to spend even one night on the Fixed Land.

At first thought this may seem like an odd choice of symbolic "forbidden fruit" on Lewis's part. Readers may associate a fixed land with absolutes, eternal truths, anchoring oneself in unchanging realities. And floating islands might connote the opposite—relativism, instability, being driven by the caprices of the moment. In the epistle of James, the doubter is described as being "like a wave of the sea, blown and tossed by the wind" (James 1:6). And in Spenser's Arthurian allegory *Faerie Queene,* one of Lewis's favorite books, the "Wandering Islands" are to be avoided by the righteous.

But for Lewis the emphasis is not on stability versus instability but on demanding control versus relinquishing it. Throughout *Perelandra* the recurring themes are accepting the fruit given—riding the wave instead of fighting the current, living on floating islands instead of a stable continent. These images gain added poignancy when we find them again in Lewis's memoir, *Surprised by Joy:* "With my mother's death all settled happiness, all that was tranquil and reliable, disappeared from my life. There was to be much fun, many pleasures, many stabs of joy; but no more of the old security. It was sea and islands now; the great continent had sunk like Atlantis." One rather suspects that Lewis's doctrine of learning to be carried on the wave rather than craving the fixed land may have been derived in part from his learning to accept the untimely loss of his mother.

The Green Lady learns a great deal from her discussions with Ransom, discovering, as she puts it, "I thought I was carried in the will of Him I love, but now I see that I walk in it." In her unfallen state she has an added advantage. As Lewis had envisioned Adam and Eve before their disobedience, the Green Lady is able to receive new understanding directly from Maleldil into her mind. Even though she has never traveled outside her world, she says she has received mental images of the furry *hrossa* and gawky *sorns* of Malacandra, and wishes she could see them with her "outward eyes." She also knows about the incarnation on "the silent planet," Earth.

When Ransom asks how she could know such things, she answers that Maleldil has told her, or even that he is telling her as she speaks to Ransom. She is a kind of natural mystic, and when she says she is in the presence of Maleldil, even Ransom notices something different about the landscape around them, a sense of fullness in the air, almost a pressure resting on his shoulders. His great task on Malacandra was to overcome his habitual fearfulness; his great task on this planet will be to overcome his habitual willfulness, to acknowledge this pressure as a Presence and to submit to a will greater than his own.

When the queen of Perelandra departs, Ransom discovers this sense of Presence is even more overpowering, seeming to squeeze out his very selfhood. Whenever he tries to assert his independence, the very air seems too full to breathe. But as he learns to surrender himself, he discovers it is not really a burden at all but rather "a sort of splendour as of eatable, drinkable, breathable gold, which fed and carried you and not only poured into you but out from you as well." As his adventure on Perelandra continues, Ransom alternates between these two moods. When he tries to assert his own will, it seems almost suffocating. But when he gives himself up, it seems a glorious fullness which makes earthly life, by comparison, seem barren and empty.

Evil does not come to Perelandra from either Ransom or the Green Lady. Rather, it arrives from outside, from the fallen planet, in the person of Weston. With the arrival of Weston, the serpent in this Eden, the contest over the Green Lady—and the fate of the planet—greatly intensifies Ransom's inner strife. Weston's philosophy has changed somewhat since his misadventures on Malacandra. Rather than the interplanetary imperialism he espoused in *Out of the Silent Planet,* he now admits of spiritual forces and sees himself as the instrument of some universal Life-Force. Though Ransom tries to warn him—"There are spirits and spirits you know"—Weston arrogantly claims that he is both the God and the devil of Christian mythology, declaring grandiosely, "I call that Force into me completely." The darkest of all spirits obliges him, causing Weston to lose his selfhood, probably also his life. His body becomes a demonized corpse: the man becomes "Un-man."

Weston, later the Un-man, plies the Green Lady with arguments for disobeying Maleldil far more subtle than anything the Eve of Genesis had to face. His recurring theme is that staying on the Fixed Land would be only superficially disobedient to Maleldil, that in asserting a self-will, making herself a "little Maleldil," she would actually be pleasing him. Try as he might to refute the Un-man's devious arguments, Ransom fears that he is not up to the job and that the Green Lady will eventually succumb.

With the Green Lady and her planet nearing a crisis, Ransom becomes physically and emotionally exhausted. After many long days and nearly sleepless nights (the Un-man doesn't sleep), he reaches the end of his resources. His "dark night of the soul" comes literally at night, as he sits alone in the dark in a state very near despair. *This can't go on,* he thinks to himself repeatedly as he enters into an internal debate every bit as fierce, protracted and theologically subtle as any of his contests with the Un-man. This dialogue between the God-will and the I-will touches on fundamental questions of Christian theology—free will versus determinism; the seeming absence of God; how a good God could allow evil and suffering in his creation.

Throughout this inner debate, one side of Ransom demands some reasonable explanation for this sorry state of affairs, and the other side is willing to trust Maleldil even in the face of seeming failure. His "voluble self" asks why Maleldil sends no miracle to save this world, why he is absent at such a critical juncture. As an answer he suddenly senses "as if the solid darkness about him had spoken with articulate voice" that Maleldil is not absent, that "the darkness was packed quite full." At that moment one side of Ransom is "prostrated in a hush of fear and love that resembled a kind of death." But Lewis's narrator comments that such "inner silence" is difficult to achieve for humans, that there is an earthbound part of the self that continues to "chatter on even in the holiest of places."

When one side of Ransom, listening to the "silence and the darkness," realizes that he himself is the miracle, the other side replies that it is all nonsense, that he "with his ridiculous piebald body and his ten times defeated arguments—what sort of miracle was that?" Why allow the fate of a world to hinge on the decisions of this "man of straw"?

Eventually, it occurs to Ransom that his mission might not be to outargue Weston but to destroy the "managed corpse" being animated by a devil. At first he considers it ridiculous to "degrade spiritual warfare to the condition of mere mythology." But then he recognizes that the earthly distinction between myth and fact is a result of the Fall, that the incarnation brought the two together again, a historical event which enacted the great myth of the dying god who lays down his life to redeem his people. Ransom does not consider this discovery simply the result of his own insight: "All this he had thought before. Now he knew it. The Presence in the darkness, never before so formidable, was putting these truths into his hands like terrible jewels."

Ransom's "voluble self" revolts at the idea of physical combat with the Un-man and continues offering up one objection after another. But "the terrible silence" around him begins to seem more and more like a face, the sad face of one waiting for him to exhaust his complaints and evasions. Once his inner rebel is silenced, Ransom assumes he will probably be killed doing battle with a "mechanized corpse." Then he hears a "Voice in the night" that tells him, "It is not for nothing you are named Ransom," adding, "My name also is Ransom." Once he is truly willing to give up his life in obedience, Ransom can hear a voice, directing and comforting him, where earlier there had only been a fullness in the air and then a Presence in the darkness and finally a kind of face.

In determining to silence the Un-man once and for all, Ransom is casting his whole force of will toward the side of his divided personality who trusts in Maleldil. Once this decision is made, Ransom finds a peace he had not yet known on this planet. On the morning he awakens resolved to do battle with the Un-man, he discovers that the piebaldness of his body has largely faded away.

The Un-man proves to be no stronger than an ordinary human of Weston's size and build, but it is seemingly a good deal harder to kill. After several vicious rounds of boxing, wrestling and clawing on one of the floating islands, there is a long sea chase and a descent into a subterranean cave. The two become separated in the dark and Ransom climbs up a sheer rock face, until he discovers a fiery underground cavern. There the Un-man accosts him one last time, filling Ransom with sudden fear. Wondering if somehow the Un-man is able to manipulate his thoughts, Ransom cries in a rage, "Get out of my brain. It isn't yours, I tell you!" Then, invoking the Trinity, he hurls a stone at the Un-man and does away with him once and for all. After this long-sought victory Ransom climbs some more until he finds a passage to the surface, reemerging on top of a high mountain, a place of brilliant flowers and singing voices in the air. There he rests beside a pool for several days, trying to regain his strength and recover from his wounds. His back is shredded as if he has been scourged, but his most serious wound is on his heel.

The culminating fight scene is quite a bit more prolonged than most readers expect, taking up almost a fifth of the novel. Obviously, Lewis has more in mind than just dispatching the villain of his story. As the story reaches its climax, it seems less about external combat and more about divisions in the "Otherworld" of Ransom's consciousness. In this section Weston, or what is left of him, seems a kind of anti-self of Ransom, a projection of Ransom's own doubts and misgivings. Several times a pathetic Westonesque voice emanates from the Un-man, not at all the pompous, unfeeling scientist, but a frightened, petulant whine uttering gibberish about fears and petty grievances stretching back to boyhood.

Ransom never knows if this is a diabolical trick from the one who absorbed Weston's personhood or if it is the actual residue of Weston's decaying psyche. But the fearful, egocentric babblings of the Weston-voice seem uncommonly like a demented version of the complaints Ransom has been hearing from his own "voluble self"—the demand for an explanation, the self-pity, the tireless ego asserting its rights.

Thus the protracted fight scene is less about hand-to-hand combat than it is about Ransom's final act of purification, his ultimate conquest of self. In destroying the Un-man, Ransom is defeating as well that side of himself that might have prevented him from accomplishing his mission on Perelandra. (The fact that this last confrontation occurs in a maze of underground caverns certainly reinforces the sense that the conflict is to be seen, at one level, as a battle within the deeper reaches of the mind.)

Readers familiar with Dante will also recognize the fight scene in *Perelandra* as Ransom's final stage of purgation, as it frequently parallels the final cantos of the *Purgatorio*. At the age of eighteen, long before he became a Christian, the young Lewis pronounced the final quarter of the *Purgatorio* to be the "heart of the whole book." And this is the section Lewis would later draw on so freely in the final quarter of *Perelandra*.

In the culminating scenes of Dante's book the narrator climbs a steep slope, fearfully crosses through a wall of fire and emerges outside upon the Garden of Earthly Delights, an unspoiled Eden. There he hears angelic voices, regales his eyes in dazzling flowers and bathes in the waters of healing and forgetfulness. Only after that final stage of purification on what he calls the holy mountain ("santo monte") is Dante ready to move on to his vision of paradise. In Dante's understanding, purgatory is not a place of punishment but of cleansing, what Evelyn Underhill calls "the privilege, the dreadful joy" of removing all vestiges of self that might "stain the white radiance of eternity." Lewis was sympathetic to this view of purgation, comparing the soul to a ragged urchin who wishes to be scrubbed (even if it hurts) and dressed in clean clothes before an audience with a king. Lewis's frequent borrowings from Dante in this and the following scene certainly underscore the idea that the last quarter of the novel is less about Weston's defeat than about Ransom's progress in his soul journey.

Of course, Ransom's wounded heel and the Un-man's crushed head remind us also of the Bible, the Redeemer promised in Genesis 3:15 who will atone for Adam's sin by crushing the serpent's head after being wounded by him. Indeed Ransom's adventure on Perelandra offers a number of parallels with Christ's mission on earth. He enters a world in order to fulfill God's purpose for it; he is tempted to give up his mission; he undergoes a kind of Gethsemane of anxiety and loneliness the night before he must suffer; he experiences a symbolic death and rebirth in being dragged below the surface and spending three days there; he re-emerges to have his mission celebrated by others; and finally he returns to his former sphere. To a reader who asked if Ransom was meant as an allegorical representation of Christ, Lewis replied that Ransom played the role of Christ in that world, not in an allegorical sense but because "in reality every real Christian is really called upon in some measure to *enact* Christ."

The final section of *Perelandra* is even more symbolic than the fight scene, and the closing pages of the book contain a mystical vision as vivid and compelling as anything in Dante. Impelled by some inner guide Ransom descends from the mountain and climbs an even steeper one called the "holy mountain." He sees an angel with a flaming sword, like the one who guarded Eden, but knows he is not meant to turn back.

He feels by then that climbing has become "not a process, but a state, and in that state of life he was content." He feels no weariness in his ascent and wonders if he might be on some "trans-mortal journey." Finally, he reaches the summit and meets the archangels of Malacandra and Perelandra, who take the form of darting pillars filled with eyes, then great slow-rolling wheels, and finally gigantic human forms, like the gods Mars and Venus. Next Ransom witnesses the coronation of the king and queen of that planet, and hears an angelic litany on the wondrous and ineffable qualities of Maleldil. Eventually, the sounds turn to sights, and he sees the "Great Dance" of the cosmos as a kaleidoscopic circle of incandescent images (much like the inviolate Rose in Dante's *Paradiso*). Finally, his mission accomplished, Ransom bids farewell to the newly enthroned king and queen and begins his journey through the heavens back to Earth.

The culminating scene of the novel contains a great deal of mystical theology expressed in poetic language and imagery. The holy mountain, the angel with a flaming sword and the seraphim—all eyes and wheels—may all be found in the *Purgatorio*. (Both Dante and Lewis acknowledged that their descriptions of seraphim drew directly on the book of Ezekiel.)

The vision of the Great Dance of the cosmos is a picture of the medieval worldview that writers of that era often used themselves. Though we have become accustomed since Newton's time to thinking of the universe as essentially a mechanism, the medieval picture was much more festive. Lewis noted in one of his lectures on medieval cosmologists that their symbol for the primum mobile was a young girl dancing and shaking a tambourine. He explains that the orderly movements of the heavenly spheres in the medieval picture "are to be conceived not as those of a machine or even an army, but rather as a dance, a festival, a symphony, a ritual, a carnival, or all of these in one." Ransom's vision in *Perelandra* is very much in this spirit, a kind of solemn and sacred revelry. As Lewis noted elsewhere, festivity is a respite from labor in our fallen world, but the "serious business of heaven" is simply the fullest possible expression of Joy.

In the Great Dance of Ransom's vision, beasts, humans and spirits all find their place; fallen worlds and unfallen ones, ancient ones and new ones, each participate in the glad ceremony. In the celestial litany that accompanies it, one angelic voice proclaims of Maleldil, "(all of Him dwells) within the seed of the smallest flower and is not cramped; Deep Heaven is inside Him who is inside the seed and does not distend Him. Blessed be He!" Another voice explains that in the Great Dance all is at the center, whether the dust or beasts or humans or gods, for "where Maleldil is, there is the center." A third cries that if not for life's great enigmas, "we should have in our minds no likeness of the Abyss of the Father, into which if a creature drop down his thoughts forever he shall hear no echo return to him. Blessed, blessed, blessed be He!"

The exclamations heard during the Great Dance frequently echo declarations by mystical writers whom Lewis knew well. Bonaventure maintained that "God is in all, and all is in God. His center is everywhere, and his circumference nowhere." Jacob Boehme wrote that if we conceive a circle "as small as a grain of mustard seed, yet the heart of God is wholly and perfectly therein." And for those born in God, he said, "the whole Heart of God is undivided." And John Ruysbroeck spoke of the "unplumbed Abyss of God."

If the Great Dance tableau of *Perelandra* is mystical, so is Ransom's response to it. As he watches, everything in the cosmos, from a momentary spark to the lifespan of a star, shines out as a circle of swirling ribbons of interwoven light. The vision becomes three-dimensional, then four-dimensional and continues adding dimension upon dimension, until "the part of him which could reason and remember dropped farther and farther behind the part of him which saw." Finally Ransom's vision reaches a "zenith of complexity" that melds into an utter "simplicity beyond all comprehension," which draws him "with cords of infinite desire into its own stillness." At the end of his vision Ransom is caught up into "a quietness, a privacy, and a freshness" that stands "farthest from our ordinary mode of being."

Feeling utterly free of encumbrances and contradictions, Ransom suddenly has a sensation of awakening. He wonders if it is still morning but discovers he has actually been enraptured for one whole year on Venus, time enough for the planet to complete its circle around the sun and stand again where it stood when his vision began. After such an enthralling vision there is little more to be said. As Ransom lies down in his coffin-shaped spacecraft, he receives a fitting benediction from the newly crowned king of Perelandra: "The splendour, the love, and the strength be upon you."

THAT HIDEOUS STRENGTH

When we meet Ransom again in the third book of the trilogy, *That Hideous Strength,* he has become a *unitive* mystic, someone whose I-will has been utterly subdued and who "walks with God." After his odyssey on other worlds, both outward and inward, he has achieved that state of spiritual equilibrium described by Underhill as one of "peaceful joy, enhanced powers, and intense certitude."

Underhill also makes it clear that the life of a unitive mystic is not one of isolated contemplation but rather one of active engagement: Bernard of Clairvaux, Hildegard of Bingen, Teresa of Ávila and John of the Cross were all among the most influential church leaders of their generation. Despite his injured heel, Ransom too provides crucial leadership. He heads a small group who have been commissioned to foil a demonic scheme to set up a totalitarian world regime in the name of sociological efficiency and technological advancement.

Ransom is not the central character in *That Hideous Strength.* Novels, at least those of the sort Lewis wrote, require protagonists who grapple with external conflicts and even more with ardent conflicts in their own hearts and minds. Ransom, however, has reached such a state of spiritual rest that no such tension saps his inner strength.

When Ransom does appear in *That Hideous Strength,* it is usually with a strong mystical aura. Early in the story we learn that he received his commission to engage in spiritual warfare here on Earth from "the great native Christian mystic whom you may have heard of—the Sura." Lewis scholar Kathryn Lindskoog has made a compelling case that the Sura mentioned here is based on a real Christian mystic from India called the *Sadhu,* "the holy one." Like the Sura, Sadhu Sundar Singh was a Christian mystic born in India and well known in England, and he disappeared under mysterious circumstances.

Lewis owned a book on the life and teachings of the Sadhu, and he carefully marked passages on Singh's mystical vision of Christ and on his discussion of the "Dark Night of the Soul." Lewis also underlined a number of the Sadhu's sayings that sound rather "Lewisian," such as the remark: "Other religions say, 'Do good and you will become good.' Christianity says, 'Be in Christ, and you will do good.' " Though Lewis's term *Sura* means "a god" in Sanskrit, not "holy one," the details he offers in *That Hideous Strength* all point to the Sadhu.

Besides being commissioned for his task by a mystic, Ransom's titles of pendragon and fisher-king also carry strong mystical overtones. In Arthurian tradition the pendragon is the head of all the armies in times of war. The most well-known of pendragons was, of course, King Arthur himself. (*Pendragon* is from Celtic "head of a dragon," taken from the dragon's head pictured on the standard of the one who held the title.) Lewis imagines that the title has been passed down secretly from generation to generation and that it now rests on the one appointed to lead the battle against a new type of invader. Ransom is also called Mr. Fisher-King, a name he took from his sister in India, who had been a friend of the Sura. In Arthurian lore, the Fisher-King is the keeper of the grail, a godlike figure with an unhealable wound.

In *That Hideous Strength* Ransom is portrayed holding court in a sky-blue upper room, with a youthful appearance despite his full golden beard, and a serene expression despite the paroxysms of pain from his wounded heel. He is compared to both a priest and a king, and those who meet him for the first time experience the same kind of holiness and majesty he himself experienced on first recognizing empty space as the empyrean "Heavens."

At the end of *That Hideous Strength* we learn that Ransom is not destined to die but will be carried back to Perelandra when his work on Earth is over. There he will journey to the mystic isle of Avalon to be with an earlier pendragon, King Arthur. Since the second book of the trilogy suggests that Perelandra is the true source of all myths of paradise, it is only fitting that Avalon should be found there and that Ransom should be healed on the world where he was wounded.

Though the three books of the Ransom trilogy make for good reading on the level of simple adventure, they also trace the inner adventure of the mystic way. When we first meet him, Ransom is a good but ordinary man who seeks nothing more than a restful holiday. But through an act of kindness toward a simple-minded boy, he sets forth on a pilgrimage that carries him to other worlds and to the very foundations of his spiritual being.

Evelyn Underhill wrote that the great goal of every mystic is complete self-surrender. Ransom achieves that goal, but only by undergoing a kind of mystical death and resurrection. By the trilogy's end the Pedestrian has become the pendragon, conversing with angels and going to rest alongside a legendary king. As his journey nears its end, Ransom is living out the blessing offered him by the unfallen Adam of Perelandra: "The splendour, the love, and the strength be upon you."

~ *Five* ~

FINDING WORDS TO
EXPLORE THE MIND OF GOD

*A*fter Elwin Ransom returns from his adventures on Perelandra, he has trouble explaining to his friends what it was like to have lived on a planet paradise. When one of them speculates incautiously that the whole experience must have been "too vague for you to put into words," Ransom replies sharply that the problem is just the opposite: "On the contrary, it is words that are too vague. The reason why the thing can't be expressed is that it's too *definite* for language." Surely, Ransom is speaking for the author in this passage. For Lewis makes much the same point in *Miracles:* "If God exists at all, He is the most concrete thing there is, the most individual. . . . He is unspeakable not by being indefinite but by being too definite for the unavoidable vagueness of language."

Here Lewis touches on one of the recurring themes of Christian mysticism: the inadequacy of language to describe God or even one's experience of God. One of William James's four defining traits of mysticism was *ineffability,* the failure of words to do justice to a sense of overwhelming encounter. James compares the mystic to an iron rod being moved back and forth by a magnet. Were it conscious, the rod would feel invisible forces at work that it would be utterly unable to explain to nearby nonmetallic objects.

As mentioned in chapter three, negative theology, emphasizing how little can be known or said about God, is most closely associated with Pseudo-Dionysius (see pp. 67-68). But it is a theme that recurs through-out the tradition of Christian mysticism. Meister Eckhart asked, "Why prate of God? Whatever you say of him is untrue." John of the Cross felt that "the soul can never attain the heights of the Divine through the medium of forms and figures." Catherine of Genoa (1447-1510) said she had learned "in one instant what words cannot express." And Lewis himself quoted several early church fathers describing God as "incomprehensible" and "inexpressible, unthinkable, invisible to created beings."

Of course, it is not only mystics who grapple with the difficulty of finding the right images or words to explain their experience of God. Throughout the Bible there are frequent references to the poverty of human thought and language to describe the richness of the Divine. The book of Job exclaims, "How great is God—beyond our understanding! / The number of his years is past finding out." And the psalmist declares, "Great is the LORD and most worthy of praise; / his greatness no one can fathom." The prophet Isaiah reminds us that God's thoughts are not our thoughts, that his ways are as far above ours as the heavens are above the earth.

Even after the fuller disclosures recorded in the Gospels, there are frequent references in the New Testament to truths beyond utterance. Paul affirmed that he had encountered Christ in person and that mysteries hidden in former ages had been revealed to him by the Spirit. Yet he too emphasized the inscrutability of the divine nature. In his epistles Paul speaks of God's "indescribable gift," "the unsearchable riches of Christ," "the peace of God, which transcends all understanding" and "the mystery of godliness." And he counts himself among those who see in a glass darkly, who know only in part.

THE IDEA OF THE HOLY

If these assertions found throughout the Bible and church tradition are taken at face value, then how can Christians claim to know the unknowable and express the inexpressible? To address this question Lewis recommended Rudolf Otto's *The Idea of the Holy* (1923) as a starting point. Otto is the scholar who coined the term *numinous,* which he defined as a person's sense of overwhelming smallness and contingency in the face of "that which is supreme above all creatures." Otto argued that rational descriptions of God (as spirit, all-powerful, all good, etc.) are necessary but incomplete, that we must also factor in some nonrational or transrational elements that are consistently evoked when mystics talk about direct encounters with the Divine.

In *The Idea of the Holy* Otto argued that the Absolute is "Wholly Other," that it can only be studied in terms of its effect on those who come into its presence. Otto identified six key markers of numinous experiences:

- Fear, awe, holy dread: "The fear of the Lord"
- Fascination, attraction, yearning
- "Majestas": a sense of ineffable magnitude
- Energy, urgency, intense dynamism, like stored-up electricity
- Wonder, astonishment, stupefaction
- Mystery, absolute unapproachability

Lewis found the term *numinous* very helpful in describing mystical experiences such as those found in the Bible and Christian mystical tradition. He also made good use of the term in *The Problem of Pain,* where he offers his own version of progressive revelation. In that book Lewis argues that human understanding of the Divine has evolved from earliest times until the crystallizing moment in history, the incarnation. Quoting Otto and adding many examples of his own, Lewis states that all cultures have left records of numinous experiences, showing their awareness of transcendent power and might. But the Old Testament offers the first clear recognition that the almighty One is also the holy One, that the numinous and the ethical emanate from the same Source. In the New Testament comes the final revelation that the righteous God is also an atoning God, suffering with and for humanity in order to redeem it.

Though Lewis quoted from *The Idea of the Holy* and recommended it often, he felt Otto went too far in defining the Absolute as "Wholly Other." For if God were *wholly* Other, we would not be able to learn the least thing about him. (Otto may have been tempted toward overstatement by the musicality of the phrase in German: *Ganz Andere.*) Lewis preferred to say that God is "Unimaginably or Insupportably Other," emphasizing that reason and imagination must always fall short in their attempts to encompass the Divine.

Yet Lewis was willing to let reason and imagination carry him as far as they could, even recognizing their ultimate limitations. When a skeptic once asked him what exactly we mean by the term *God,* Lewis replied without hesitation, "God is a self-subsistent Being, cause of Himself." Of course, he recognized that such a formal definition barely scratched the surface of the question. Yet Lewis always sought to supplement apophatic, or negative theology, with cataphatic, or positive theology. In *Surprised by Joy* Lewis characteristically balances the two approaches, admitting how little we can truly plumb the depths of the Divine, yet realizing we must do the best we can with what tools we have: "Into the region of awe, in deepest solitude there is a road right out of the self, a commerce with . . . the naked Other, imageless (though our imagination salutes it with a hundred images), unknown, undefined, desired."

Lewis's phrase about the imagination trying to salute "the naked Other" with a hundred images clearly shows his fascination with how finite human minds might try to envision the Infinite. Christian mystics often resort to poetry and paradox to evoke their experience of God. Pseudo-Dionysius spoke of the "welcoming silence of the dazzling darkness." Hildegard of Bingen described God as "the Living Light" and Jan van Ruysbroek (1293-1381) wrote about the "Wayless Way" and the "Teeming Desert." Mechthild of Magdeburg made whole hymns out of names for God:

> O burning Mountain, O chosen Sun,
> O perfect Moon, O fathomless Well,
> O unattainable Height, O Clearness beyond measure,

O Wisdom without end, O Mercy without limit,
O Strength beyond resistance, O Crown beyond all majesty:
The humblest thing you created sings your praise.

Most Christians are willing to settle for images of God taken from the Bible—God as the Ancient of Days, a king on his throne, a shepherd and so forth. But the Bible is not self-interpreting, and some of its writers offer contrasting pictures of God. The book of Hebrews stresses the changelessness of God's nature, that he is "the same yesterday and today and forever" (13:8). But several Old Testament passages portray God in much more human terms, subject to changing human impulses and passions.

Two recurring issues in biblical interpretation are *anthropomorphism,* picturing God in human form, and *anthropopathism,* trying to interpret the divine mind in terms of human emotions. One can see an example of the first in Genesis 3:8, which says that the Lord God walked in the garden of Eden "in the cool of the day." In the ancient Middle East, it was customary to walk outdoors in the early morning, before the intense midday heat set in. But presumably the Creator, the star-maker, he who swirls out galaxies like so many spirals of cosmic cotton candy, would not have to worry about the heat of the noonday sun. In this small detail the writer of Genesis seems to be visualizing God as a Middle Eastern monarch, not as Master of the universe.

Perhaps a more serious problem in constructing a coherent theology is anthropopathism, attributing human emotions to God. In Exodus 32, for example, God threatens to destroy the Israelites for creating a golden calf and worshiping it. But Moses intercedes for his people and asks the Lord whether he wants the Egyptians to think God took the Israelites out into the desert only to wipe them off the face of the earth. At this reminder God seems to change his mind and "relent[s]" (Exodus 32:14; the KJV and RSV put the case even more strongly, saying, "And the LORD repented of the evil which he thought to do unto [to] his people"). This passage in Exodus gives the impression that God was on the verge of a rash and violent act and had to be calmed down by a mere human being, Moses.

Most conservative Christian scholars interpret episodes like this one in terms of progressive revelation, viewing a particular passage in the context of the whole Bible, interpreting Old Testament portraits of God in the light of the fuller revelation provided in the New Testament. Paul himself suggests the idea of progressive revelation in the book of Ephesians, where he talks about "the mystery of Christ, which was not made known to men in other generations as it has now been revealed by the Spirit to God's holy apostles and prophets" (3:4-5). Some modernist interpreters take this to an extreme, trying to banish any portrayal of God in human terms, referring instead to a "Life Force" or a "Ground of Being."

For Lewis the opposite errors to be avoided are those of excessive anthropomorphism, picturing God too much as if he were a man, and excessive abstraction, trying to avoid pictures altogether. He argued that you cannot think clearly about God until you have examined more carefully the nature of human thought and human language. Lewis notes that the Christian worldview may seem somewhat quaint or naive to some modern readers, with its seeming commitment to a three-story universe, with heaven above, hell below and earth in the middle. Instead of saying "God came down to earth," which makes it sound as if he sits on a throne in a sky palace, a modern theologian might prefer to say "God entered into history." But Lewis notes that this only substitutes one metaphor for another: vertical descent for some less well-defined horizontal movement. Likewise, modern thinkers may try to avoid anthropomorphism by describing God as a Life Force or a Ground of Being. But these are again metaphors, conjuring up impersonal images of gravity or electricity or the earth beneath our feet. For Lewis, these are actually weaker metaphors than anthropomorphic ones since they leave out consciousness, intelligence, goodness and other traits fundamental to God's nature. He tells of a young girl raised to believe in God as a "perfect substance." In her mind the phrase called forth the image of a vast tapioca pudding—and she wasn't at all fond of tapioca!

Lewis concluded that we must always distinguish between thinking and imagining, between concepts and the images in which they are clothed. We should understand from the outset that all theological language is necessarily metaphorical and that metaphors and models are ultimately inadequate. The safest course, according to Lewis, is to accept the authority of scriptural imagery since "it comes to us from writers who were closer to God than we, and it has withstood the test of Christian experience down the centuries." He adds that we should always keep in mind that any given metaphor needs to be balanced and complemented by others. Lewis recommends a phrase he borrowed from his friend Charles Williams. For every picture of God, we must acknowledge, "This is also Thou; neither is this Thou." For example, the image of God as a friend or lover may be helpful as far as it goes, but we must also recall the scene in Revelation where John, on first seeing Christ, falls down at Christ's feet as if John were dead (see Revelation 1:17). In general, Lewis wonders if the greater danger for modern minds is abstraction, not anthropomorphism. "What soul," he asks, "ever perished for believing that God the Father really has a beard?"

Having distinguished between ideas and images, Lewis goes further in distinguishing between different kinds of images. He says it is important to notice the difference between metaphors we use merely to illustrate a point and those we actually need to think with (master's metaphors versus pupil's metaphors). To give a contemporary example, a physics teacher might draw an atom on the blackboard as an electron orbiting the nucleus, like a miniature solar system. She knows that electrons don't actually circle nuclei the way planets circle the sun, but it is a useful device for explaining chemical elements, molecular bonds and so on. But when that same physicist talks about quanta, the elemental units of energy, as both waves and particles, she is not trying to be paradoxical or inventing a teaching device. These are the only analogies she has, however contradictory and inadequate, to visualize subatomic entities that have no parallels in our everyday world.

The same distinction applies at the macrocosmic level as at the microcosmic. Again, we are moving outside the frame of the everyday world and must resort to metaphors, some of which we can see behind and some of which we cannot. When the psalmist calls God his "shield," the basic idea is protection (see Psalm 18:2). We might substitute other metaphors such as God as a rock or God as a fortress to convey the same idea. (Indeed, the psalmist uses these metaphors in the same verse where God is called a shield.)

But when Christian creeds speak of God the Father and God the Son, there is no easy way to see behind this model. Lewis notes that some thinkers are uncomfortable with the biological analogy—it is hard to understand how spirit begets spirit or how one eternal person could seem to be younger than another one. But in trying to visualize the first two persons of the Trinity in other terms, such as light from a lamp or heat from a flame, we seem to speak of only one thing, not two, and so lose an essential part of the concept. In the final analysis it is better to accept the metaphors given us in the Bible and church creeds, however elusive, than to try to invent new metaphors that will prove, on closer inspection, to be even more problematic. On a typically platonic note, Lewis observes that this whole "problem" of comprehending the Trinity actually puts the case backward:

> Grammatically, the things we say of Him are "metaphorical": but in a deeper sense it is our physical and psychic energies that are "metaphors" of the real Life which is God. Divine Sonship is, so to speak, the solid of which biological sonship is merely a diagrammatic representation on the flat.

DIVINE LOVE AND DIVINE WRATH

Lewis seems to have borrowed his distinction between metaphors we teach with and metaphors we need to think with from Edwyn Bevan's *Symbolism and Belief* (1938), a book he often recommended and which he quoted in *The Problem of Pain* and *Miracles*. Bevan builds on Otto's discussion of the numinous, advising that we think very carefully about the metaphors we choose to describe the divine nature. Surveying world religions Bevan notes that deity is most often associated with images of height, agelessness and, especially, dazzling light. (Of this last trait Bevan notes epigrammatically, "The numinous is luminous.")

Bevan focuses especially on the issue of anthropopathism, analogies between human emotions and the divine mind. He notes that divine love and divine wrath are sometimes seen as different sides of the same coin, but he argues they are actually very different sorts of metaphors.

In all symbols, explains Bevan, one thing stands for another. In some cases the symbol is a simplified but essentially accurate picture of the thing. In others it is a somewhat contrived attempt to evoke something that is itself beyond words or images. A painting of a tree is a pictorial symbol of an actual tree. It is smaller and two-dimensional, but it gives a general sense of the tree's shape, color and texture. But if a blind person asks you to describe the color scarlet, you might say, "It's rather like a blast of trumpets." You are hoping your listener will catch the idea of something that dramatically arrests the attention. But if your blind hearer thinks you mean scarlet is somehow musical or metallic, you have failed completely to convey the quality of the color.

Bevan argues that it is crucial to distinguish between symbols we can "see behind" (translate into concepts) and those we cannot. He says that God's love is the first type of symbol. Human loves, especially the more stable, enduring kinds like a mother's love, offer a useful sketch of divine love. Jesus himself invited the comparison when he told his disciples, "Love one another as the Father has loved you."

What we call divine wrath, though, according to Bevan, is much more like trying to explain scarlet to a blind person. When a soul is mired in self and moving away from God, there are terrible consequences. It is somewhat like the tragic things that can happen when one person is uncontrollably angry with another. But wrath is a transient emotion, usually the result of a human's thwarted will, and it may be misleading to impute this trait too literally to the divine nature, which is "the same yesterday and today and forever."

Bevan's observation is certainly supported by the tradition of Christian mysticism. If we peruse a collection of classic Christian sermons, we might find the topics of divine love and divine wrath covered in about equal proportions. For every comforting word about grace or forgiveness, we are likely to find a word of warning about the coming day of judgment. But for mystics the great and overwhelming reality is that of divine love. From their direct encounters with God, they come away with a sense of peace and rest, not dread. They ardently seek greater purity, not to appease an angry God but rather to be more like the One whose dazzling righteousness they have sensed directly. Julian of Norwich came away from her divine "showings" with a vivid reassurance that all human ills are finite, whereas God's love is infinite: "All shall be well, all shall be well, all manner of things shall be well." For Julian death, illness, pain and everything else will be swallowed up in victory. And after one of her mystical ecstasies Catherine of Genoa proclaimed, "If one drop of what I feel could be dropped into hell, then hell would be transformed into Paradise."

In keeping with Bevan's distinction and with the overwhelming consensus of Christian mystics, Lewis does not treat love and wrath as equal but opposite attributes in the divine nature. Rather he uses love as a synonym for God, "the Love that made the worlds." By contrast, he places the term *wrath* in quotation marks, calling it "a corollary of divine goodness." In so doing Lewis is not offering up a modernized "Christianity lite," shorn of its hard sayings about judgment and condemnation. Rather he asks his readers to ponder more deeply the meaning of judgment and condemnation in the context of an all-loving, self-giving God.

"God is love." The Bible phrase is so familiar, Lewis notes, that readers may not consider its full implications. For one thing, it does not simply mean "God loves human beings." For there was a time when human beings did not exist, but that did not alter the character of God. Borrowing a phrase from Augustine, Lewis says that "in the land of the Trinity," love is uncreated and eternal: "The Father delights in His Son; the Son looks up to His Father." And in this bond of love beyond time is the Spirit, another person uniting "begetting love" and "love begotten." Those who argue that God *needed* to create human beings to offer God love and adoration have not considered fully the utter self-sufficiency of the triune God. At the very foundation of being is an eternal fellowship.

Lewis also notes that "God is love" means more than "God has loving feelings towards his creatures." In humans love is a passion that can wax and wane, which can die out altogether. But God is not subject to passions; he is not affected by love, because he *is* love. His love never wearies or falters, never seeks anything less in the beloved than a purity of spirit that can return his unwavering love. In Lewis's analogy we may get wet by going into water; but God does not get wet because he *is* water. His love has all the intensity of human passions, and more, but none of their changefulness. God does not simply love, for "God is love."

What then is the wrath of a loving God? As Lewis explains it, "Love may forgive all infirmities and love still in spite of them: but love cannot cease to will their removal. Love is more sensitive than hatred itself to every blemish in the beloved. . . . Of all powers he forgives most, but condones least." Quoting George MacDonald, Lewis says that God is "easy to please, but hard to satisfy." In this view, the wrath of God is a symbol of the "unappeasable distaste" in a perfect Being for that which is not perfect, a consuming fire of purification.

In humans wrath is a passion, usually an intense flare-up at having our pride injured or our will denied. In the Divine, wrath is the ongoing response of goodness to the presence of badness, and a will that humans should recognize that badness for themselves. If a mother shouts to her son to get away from a hornet's nest, the urgency in her voice may be indistinguishable from anger. If the boy ignores his mother's warning and gets stung, his pain is very real. But his suffering is not a *punishment* for his heedlessness but rather a *consequence* of his actions.

Of course, Lewis was resolutely orthodox. He did not mean for his understanding of divine wrath to challenge biblical teaching or church creeds. References to "the coming wrath" and those who are storing up wrath for themselves occur most often in the books of Romans and Revelation, but the focus is on the *objects* of wrath, people who don't repent and who face judgment, not on wrath as a passion in the divine nature.

In fact, the word is sometimes (as in Romans 13:5 NIV) translated simply "punishment," without any reference to an emotional state.

In looking at what are called "terror" sermons in church history, we can't help but notice how often the speakers themselves are angry or else concerned about their loss of political or social clout. In the sixteenth century, Protestant and Roman Catholic divines frequently invoked the wrath of God against each other, often assuming those on the other side had forfeited their salvation. In colonial New England the Puritans were usually in the minority and anxious lest secular fellow colonists undermine their theocratic experiment. Michael Wigglesworth's apocalyptic "Day of Doom" (1662) and Jonathan Edwards's "Sinners in the Hands of an Angry God" (1741) seem designed in part to intimidate the Puritans' worldly minded neighbors who might be more interested in profits than prophets. A similar hellfire sermon may be found in James Joyce's novel *A Portrait of the Artist as a Young Man,* where the local priest offers grisly details about the tortures of the damned. Joyce suggests the priest is less concerned about the souls of his young parishioners than he is about how many of them are leaving the church. Admittedly, these examples are anecdotal and spread centuries apart. But we shouldn't be surprised if a more systematic survey of "terror" sermons throughout church history took as its title "God in the Hands of Angry Sinners."

There is a notable difference of emphasis in the literature of Christian mysticism. In the fourteenth century Julian of Norwich declared, "I saw no wrath but on man's part: and that forgiveth He in us. For wrath is naught else but a contrariness to peace and love, which is a failing not in God but on our part." In the eighteenth century William Law made a similar point about fallen angels in *An Appeal to All Who Doubt* (a treatise Lewis pronounced one of the best religious books he'd ever read):

> God darts no more anger at angels when fallen, than He did in the creation of them: they are not in Hell because Father, Son, and Holy Ghost are angry at them, and so cast them into a punishment. They are in wrath and darkness because they have done to

the light which infinitely flows forth from God, as a man does who puts out his own eyes. He is in darkness, not because the sun has darkened towards him, but because he has put out that birth of light in himself.

In the twentieth century, Indian Christian mystic Sundar Singh explained his perception by saying simply, "God is never annoyed with anybody."

Of course, mystics speak from their own experience, and their interpretations must be assessed in the light of the Bible and received orthodox opinion. As was his habit Lewis sought the middle ground of "mere Christianity," avoiding vivid depictions of a scowling God dangling sinners over a fiery pit, but also satirizing the giddy, vacuous theology in which God is pictured as a "grandfather in heaven—a senile benevolence" presiding over a universe in which "a good time was had by all."

Lewis conceded that the doctrine of divine wrath has its place in the Bible and church tradition. Echoing Bevan's paradigm Lewis concluded that divine wrath is best understood as an analogy, yet the kind of analogy one cannot improve on. In *The Idea of the Holy* Rudolf Otto suggested that divine wrath might be better understood as an impersonal numinous force rather than the response of an offended magistrate. Otto compares this attribute to the electric shock one might receive in mishandling a live wire. As usual Lewis doubts the wisdom of trying to improve on biblical metaphors. He observes that a person can forgive, while an electric wire cannot. For Lewis the best course is to accept the *purport* of the analogy rather than trying to translate it into a concept or a different metaphor.

Of course, Lewis repeatedly emphasized that the reason for thinking through these issues is not simply to engage in abstract speculation about God but to encourage right relations with God. He felt that a fear of divine wrath was one of the most primitive of religious emotions and not the one Christians should emphasize if they want to be the fragrance of Christ to those who are perishing. Terror sermons, far from encouraging abandonment of self, make a naked appeal to self-interest and self-preservation. They also imply that the most important divine attribute is anger, as if John's famous phrase should read "God is wrath."

Lewis argued that a far more effective strategy is to show that what our souls most long for is God. He noted that the anxieties induced by a fire-and-brimstone sermon may only last a few hours. But a soul awakened to a desire for "the Mighty Beauty" begins a journey that will last a life-time—and beyond a lifetime.

DIVINE SORROW AND DIVINE JOY

In general, Christian mystics have spent less time describing divine wrath than they have pondering something that feels to them like divine sorrow. Scholar Evelyn Underhill says that when earthly mists are swept away and the "Everlasting Hills" come into view, Christian mystics often report "a splendour and adorable reality in the world," accompanied by a sense of "divine sorrow at the heart of things." Citing Francis of Assisi, Catherine of Genoa and the fourteenth-century German mystic Rulman Merswin, Underhill explains that "an intimate realization of the divine" brings with it a sense of "love and sorrow, the discord between Perfect Love and an imperfect world." In addition Hildegard of Bingen wrote about God's sense of "world-sadness," and George MacDonald specu-lated that Christ's Passion on earth may have only been a part of some greater cost he bore from the foundations of time as the eternal Son.

C. S. Lewis also wondered about sorrow as a possible dimension of the divine nature. He focused on Bible passages that seem to suggest di-vine suffering. Citing MacDonald he pondered if Christ's Passion during his time on earth was part of the eternal dynamic of the Trinity. Lewis draws our attention to verses about divine longing in both the Old and New Testaments. From Jeremiah he quotes:

"Is not Ephraim my dear son,
    the child in whom I delight?
Though I often speak against him,

I still remember him.

Therefore my heart yearns for him;

I have great compassion for him," declares the LORD. (31:20 KJV)

From Matthew's Gospel, Lewis recalls Christ's lament over the holy city: "O Jerusalem, Jerusalem, you who kill the prophets and stone those sent to you, how often I have longed to gather your children together, as a hen gathers her chicks under her wings, but you were not willing" (23:37 KJV). Lewis also notes that Christ asked Saul on the road to Damascus, "Why do you persecute me?" not "Why do you persecute my disciples?" suggesting that the Son participates in the afflictions of his people (see Acts 9:4). Later on, Paul—the former persecutor now taking his place among the most violently persecuted—warns the Ephesians not to "grieve the Holy Spirit" and reassures Christians at Rome that the Spirit intercedes for them "with groans that words cannot express" (Ephesians 4:30; Romans 8:26).

Lewis assumes that references to divine longing or grief are analogies, like allusions to divine wrath. But he goes on to speculate what it must have cost an all-good Creator to breathe life into beings who could choose between good and evil. Lewis wonders if there may have been "an anguish, an alienation, a crucifixion in the creative act," God bringing into being that which is finite, temporal, fallible, Fall-able. Lewis speculates as well that God, in withdrawing his sovereignty in order to make room for the free will of creatures made in his likeness, might be seen as a tragic Creator before he was a tragic Redeemer.

In *The Magician's Nephew* Lewis gives an imaginative embodiment to his speculation about a God who shares the affliction of his children. The lion Aslan, who enacts the role of Christ in the world of Narnia, calls on young Digory to travel to a distant garden and return with a silver apple to protect the newly created land from evil. Digory's mother back on earth is dying, and he can't help but blurt out a question to the great lion whether anything can be done for her. When he despondently raises his eyes to meet Aslan's, he receives one of the greatest surprises of his life:

For the tawny face was bent down near his own and (wonder of wonders) great shining tears stood in the Lion's eyes. They were such big, bright tears compared with Digory's own that for a moment he felt as if the Lion must really be sorrier about his Mother than he was himself. "My son, my son," said Aslan, "Grief is great. Only you and I know that in this land yet. Let us be good to one another."

Despite their shared sorrow Aslan explains that he must attend first to the safety of Narnia. He sends Digory off on a winged horse to fetch the apple that will protect that world. In a scene reminiscent of Genesis, Digory is tempted to keep the apple for himself and use it to heal his mother. But he does as he has been told and returns to Aslan with the apple. In the end Narnia is kept safe and Digory's mother is miraculously healed. Though Lewis's own mother died when he was nine years old, he suggests in his fiction that God will someday wipe away all tears and that—more than we know—he understands those tears.

In *The Magician's Nephew* Lewis also explores another mystery of the divine nature: eternal joy. When Digory returns, having resisted temptation and accomplished his mission, Aslan pronounces "Well done" in a voice that makes the whole earth shake. Digory realizes that his story will ring down through the centuries in Narnia, but he feels no conceit, only contentment to be standing face to face with Aslan. "Well done, Son of Adam," repeats the lion, a resounding commendation that washes over Digory's soul and makes him forget his sorrow. Having come from a garden paradise that felt like Eden, he now stands before Aslan in a paradise that feels like heaven.

Lewis believed that such scenes of joy were indeed "the serious business of heaven." In his classic sermon "The Weight of Glory," Lewis discusses that most sublime of accolades, the voice of God saying "Well done, thou good and faithful servant." Lewis argued that one of the great pleasures of heaven, the promised glory, will simply be to know that you have pleased God, that you have contributed to divine happiness. All earthly fame or honor pales before the thought that God will some day single out each faithful servant, express his delight as an artist for the finished work or as a father for his child. Lewis adds that "it seems impossible, a weight or burden of glory which our thoughts can hardly sustain. But so it is." In trying to plumb the depths of the divine mind, Lewis concluded that sometimes the most mystical scenes we can imagine will ultimately turn out to be those that are most real.

~ *Six* ~

MYSTICAL ELEMENTS
IN THE NARNIA CHRONICLES

Lewis explained in *Surprised by Joy* that during his adolescence the two hemispheres of his mind—intellect and imagination—were sharply divided. His imaginative side regaled in "a many-islanded sea of poetry and myth," while his logical side was dominated by "a glib and shallow rationalism." When he became a Christian, though, this spiritual schizophrenia came to an end: his intellect and imagination became powerfully integrated and mutually reinforcing. This long-sought and hard-won singleness of mind creates fascinating interconnections among Lewis's books, so that reading in any one of them can shed new light on all the others. Given his habit of grappling with theological issues both critically and creatively, it is not surprising that Lewis's interest in mysticism, mentioned so often in his essays and letters, should find imaginative expression in the Narnia Chronicles.

When Lewis began writing the Chronicles in the spring of 1949, he was not intending to write Christian fiction. Some readers have assumed that some didactic purpose was foremost in his mind when he created Narnia—that he first decided to write something Christian for children, chose the fairy tale as his vehicle and then studied theology and child psychology in order to create spiritual allegories for young readers. Lewis bluntly dismissed this view of his writing method as "pure moonshine." He explained that the process by which Narnia came into being was much more fanciful and mysterious: "Everything began with images: a faun carrying an umbrella, a queen on a sledge, a magnificent lion. At first there wasn't even anything Christian about them; that element pushed itself in of its own accord."

As the story-making process matured, however, Lewis began to see the Christian possibilities in the narratives that were beginning to take shape. He remembered how in his own childhood he lacked any genuine sense of awe or love for God simply because he felt obligated to feel a certain way, as dictated by his elders. He wondered if, by recasting essential Christian doctrines into "an imaginary world, stripping them of their stained-glass and Sunday school associations," he could "steal past those watchful dragons" of enforced reverence or oft-repeated religious lessons. By enlisting the unfettered powers of imagination, Lewis hoped to recapture the original beauty and poignancy of the good news. In this strategy, of course, Lewis succeeded brilliantly.

Despite their spiritual richness it does a great disservice to the Chronicles to read them as allegories, as if all the major characters and incidents are merely disguised Bible stories. Lewis called his children's books "supposals," not symbols or allegories, explaining to one group of young inquirers:

> You are mistaken when you think that everything in the books "represents" something in this world. Things do that in *The Pilgrim's Progress* but I'm not writing in that way. I did not say to myself "Let us represent Jesus as He really is in our world by a Lion in Narnia": I said "Let us *suppose* that there were a land like Narnia and that the Son of God, as He became a Man in our world, became a Lion there, and then imagine what would happen."

This turned out to be a fruitful supposal indeed, one which produced not one book but a complete series of seven: *The Lion, the Witch and the Wardrobe* (1950), *Prince Caspian* (1951), *The Voyage of the "Dawn Treader"* (1952), *The Silver Chair* (1953), *The Horse and His Boy* (1954), *The Ma-*

gician's Nephew (1955) and *The Last Battle* (1956). The culminating book in what his friend Roger Lancelyn Green dubbed the "Narnia Chronicles" won the prestigious Carnegie Medal for best work of children's fiction published in that year.

Most Lewis scholars agree that first-time readers of the Chronicles should read them in the order they were published so they can enjoy more fully the imaginative world of Narnia as it unfolded in Lewis's mind. However, Lewis once wrote to a little boy that he could see the logic of reading them according to "Narnian chronological time," which would be *The Magician's Nephew; The Lion, the Witch and the Wardrobe; The Horse and His Boy, Prince Caspian; The Voyage of the "Dawn Treader"; The Silver Chair;* and *The Last Battle.* Since that is the order in which the Chronicles are currently being published, that is the order in which they will be discussed here.

Just as it is a mistake to read the Chronicles as biblical allegories, it would be equally misguided to read them as mystical stories simply because Aslan physically appears in Narnia in a way that God does not appear to us in our world today. The Chronicles are better read as "incarnational fiction" than mystical fiction since most of Aslan's visits to Narnia are imaginative versions of *theophanies,* physical manifestations to groups of people, rather than mystical experiences in the consciousness of one person. When the proud horse Bree, for example, presumes to dabble in "Narnian theology," he explains that Aslan may be metaphorically considered strong as a lion or fierce as a lion, but it would be disrespectful to consider him an actual lion with paws and whiskers. Just then Aslan appears, scaring the wits and the shallow philosophy out of Bree, and commanding the cowering steed to draw near: "Do not dare not to dare. Touch me. Smell me. Here are my paws, here is my tail, these are my whiskers. I am a true Beast." As so often happens, Narnian incidents, while not allegorical, have biblical parallels. It is hard to read this scene without thinking of Christ's words to "Doubting" Thomas, inviting him to touch the wounds in his hands and his side (John 20:26-28).

Though most of the Chronicles portray Aslan incarnationally, not mystically, there are still a good many mystical overtones in the series. Throughout Lewis's classic children's stories there are echoes of biblical theophanies as well as illustrations of Rudolf Otto's ideas on the numinous, Edwyn Bevan's ideas on metaphors for the Deity and insights by medieval mystics about what they sometimes called "the journey to God."

THE MAGICIAN'S NEPHEW

Some of the most poignant scenes in all the Chronicles are the ones in which Digory learns that Aslan fully understands the meaning of human sorrows and human joys (see chap. five). In the closing chapters of *The Magician's Nephew* Lewis explores another mystical motif, coinherence, an idea he adapted from his friend Charles Williams.

When Digory is sent far into the west to find a garden on top of a steep, green hill, he discovers the apple tree he is seeking in a walled orchard. On gates of gold he finds these words inscribed in letters of silver:

Come in by the gold gates or not at all,
Take of my fruit for others or forbear.
For those who steal or those who climb my wall
Shall find their heart's desire and find despair.

Despite insidious temptations from Jadis the witch to disobey the great lion, Digory does as he has been commanded, earning that resounding "Well done!" from Aslan and guaranteeing that the newly created land of Narnia "shall have a long bright morning before any clouds come over the sun." In placing the protection of Narnia above his own heart's desire to try to heal his dying mother, Digory shows that he understands well the words written on the golden gates.

The words on the garden entry offer a poetic expression of coinherence, what Lewis preferred to call the "Principle of Vicariousness." In *Miracles* he explains that, even in the natural world, "Everything is indebted to everything else, sacrificed to everything else, dependent on everything else," whether flowers and bees or predators and prey. Lewis goes on to explain that this natural ecology finds an even higher expression in sacred history, first in the chosen people who are "chosen not for their own sake . . . but for the sake of the unchosen" and finally in the "Sinless Man [who] suffers for the sinful."

In a letter to his friend Arthur Greeves, Lewis interpreted vicarious-ness, the idea of inescapable interdependence, as not just something found in nature or history but as one of the most pervasive principles of human life:

> It [is] the rule of the universe that others can do for us what we cannot do for ourselves and one can paddle every canoe *except* one's own. That is why Christ's suffering *for us* is not a mere theo-logical dodge but the supreme case of the law that governs the whole world: and when they mocked him by saying, "He saved others, himself he cannot save" [Matthew 27:42], they were really uttering, little as they knew, the ultimate law of the spiritual world.

Spiritual laws, like the law of gravity, work whether you are aware of them or not. Digory would doubtless have had trouble with terms such as *vicariousness* or *coinherence*. But he knows enough to trust Aslan and contributes not only to the protection of Narnia but also to the miracu-lous recovery of his mother.

THE LION, THE WITCH AND THE WARDROBE

When Lewis explained Rudolf Otto's idea of the *numinous* in *The Problem of Pain,* he gave examples from the Bible, such as Jacob's dream of a lad-der to heaven (Genesis 28:17) and Ezekiel's vision of four-faced creatures and wheels full of eyes (Ezekiel 1:18). Lewis also supplied examples of uncanny longing and dread from classics such as Aeschylus, Ovid and Virgil. Amid these ancient and venerable sources Lewis included a more homely illustration, a passage from Kenneth Grahame's *The Wind in the Willows* (1908). In the scene where Rat and Mole approach the god Pan, Mole timidly asks his companion if he is afraid: " 'Afraid?' murmured the Rat, his eyes shining with unutterable love. 'Afraid? Of Him? O, never, never. And yet—and yet—O Mole, I am afraid.' "

This folksy—or furry—example of the numinous sounds very much like a scene set in Narnia. Indeed, Lewis created many such episodes in the Chronicles to evoke a sense of the numinous. The very first time the Pevensie children hear that "Aslan is on the move," they have no idea who or what Aslan is (and neither do readers if they are following the Chronicles in the order they were published). And yet the very name has a mystical aura, laying bare the very souls of the children who hear it. The word makes Peter, the eldest, feel "brave and adventurous." His sister Susan feels as if "some delicious smell or delightful strain of music had just floated by her." For the youngest, Lucy, it is like waking up to discover the summer holidays have begun. For Edmund, though, already a bully and soon to be a traitor, the very name *Aslan* induces "a sensation of mysterious horror."

Later in the story when the three loyal Pevensie children, accompanied by Mr. and Mrs. Beaver, first meet Aslan in person, the scene is highly reminiscent of the one Lewis so enjoyed from *The Wind in the Willows:* "But as for Aslan himself, the Beavers and the children didn't know what to do or say when they saw him. People who have not been in Narnia sometimes think that a thing cannot be good and terrible at the same time. If the children had ever thought so, they were cured of it now." When Aslan speaks to them in his deep, resonant voice, the children lose their anxiety and feel "glad and quiet." Throughout the Chronicles, Aslan's name, and even moreso his presence, evokes a strong sense of the numinous—a piercing delight to the spiritually healthy, a threat and a terror to those whose hearts are ensnared in selfishness and sin.

If the first mention of Aslan injects a mystical note early in *The Lion, the Witch and the Wardrobe,* his supreme sacrifice at the end of the story draws readers much further into the realm of divine mysteries. After siding with the wicked queen and betraying his siblings, Edmund learns, in the school of suffering, how foolish he has been and how cruel she truly is. But Edmund's sincere repentance, even his bravery in battle and his forgiveness by the others, are not enough to balance the moral scales of Narnia. The self-designated queen, now openly called a witch, invokes the "Deep Magic," a law engraved on the Stone Table before them: the rule that any traitor, like Edmund, must forfeit his life as her lawful prey. Aslan offers his own life for Edmund's, enduring a night of lonely sadness like Gethsemane and then a day of humiliation and death like the Passion. But beyond the Deep Magic the Witch knows about, the condemnation of law, is the Deeper Magic, Aslan's fulfilling of the law and his triumph over death.

Aslan's sacrificial death and his return to life are so artfully portrayed in *The Lion, the Witch and the Wardrobe* that many readers get swept up in the story and don't stop to ponder its biblical overtones. Pauline Baynes, the famous illustrator for the original edition of the Chronicles, confessed she was in tears while drawing this scene for the book, but its parallels with Christ's suffering didn't occur to her at the time.

Other readers may err in the opposite direction, treating these chapters in *The Lion, the Witch and the Wardrobe* as a direct expression of Lewis's theology. Some have complained that this scene offers an inadequate view of atonement because Aslan offers his life not for a fallen race but for only one person, Edmund, whose sins have already been paid for in our own world. Others wonder why Aslan would ever strike a bargain with the Witch, as God would certainly have no such dealings with the devil. Rebel angels have no legal rights, in heaven or on earth.

Lewis sometimes responded to such criticisms by offering reminders to scholars like the ones he sent to schoolchildren. To one seminarian Lewis explained, "You must not confuse my romances with my theses. In the latter I state and argue a creed. In the former much is merely supposed for the sake of the stories." Instead of trying to extract a particular theology from the climactic scenes of *The Lion, the Witch and the Wardrobe,* it may be wiser to simply acknowledge them as the most moving portrayal of vicariousness, "the Sinless who suffers for the sinful," to be found anywhere in Lewis's books.

It is intriguing, though, that Lewis should refer to Aslan's substitutionary sacrifice as the Deep Magic and his return to life as the Deeper Magic. In his theological books Lewis was disarmingly honest about doctrines he couldn't fully comprehend. He confessed in *Mere Christianity* that he believed in the doctrine of Christ's atonement, but he didn't understand it. He noted one can affirm that "Christ's death has somehow put us right with God" without subscribing to any particular theory of how this came to be. He added that we can "accept what Christ has done without knowing how it works," just as a person can be nourished by eating food without knowing the first thing about digestion. In *The Problem of Pain,* Lewis refers to the most common view of the atonement, Anselm's explanation that Christ's death was needed to satisfy divine justice. To this approach Lewis confessed that the twelfth-century theologian's views "may have done good in their day but they do no good to me." Rather than offering his own theory of the atonement, Lewis just speculates that it must be rooted in "some kind of 'inter-animation' of which we have no conception at all." These remarks suggest that Lewis was comfortable regarding a key Christian doctrine as essentially mystical, not to be dissected by rational inquiry.

Lewis also referred to the doctrine of Christ's Real Presence in the elements of Holy Communion as "strong magic." Though the word *magic* most often has negative connotations in Lewis, referring usually to human attempts to master occult forces, he sometimes resorted to that term when discussing the unfathomable mysteries of the King of heaven. In this context Lewis uses the word *magical* where most writers would use the word *mystical.* Perhaps the most important thing to remember about this form of divine "magic" is that when Lucy asks, "Can anything be done to save Edmund?" the great lion answers, "All shall be done."

THE HORSE AND HIS BOY

The Horse and His Boy is a double escape story, as the peasant boy Shasta runs away to avoid being sold into slavery while Aravis, a Calormene princess, runs away to avoid an arranged marriage with an old man she finds repulsive. Their two escapes, both on the backs of talking horses from Narnia, become one escape journey when the two riders are driven together by lions on either side of them. Shasta is later forced to separate from the other three when the party reaches the great city of Tashbaan, and he spends a lonely night among ancient tombs outside the city. There on the edge of the desert Shasta is comforted by a large cat who, in some sort of dream, seems to turn into a lion in order to frighten away jackals who have ventured dangerously close. After Shasta is reunited with his Narnian horse, Bree, and Aravis and her horse, Hwin, the four continue their journey toward "Narnia and the North." As the horses tire almost to the point of exhaustion, they find one last burst of energy, supplied by the fear of being chased by yet another lion, till finally they take refuge with a wise old mountain hermit.

Before he can take much rest, though, Shasta is sent out again, this time to warn the king of Archenland about some Calormenes who are planning a surprise attack. On his way there Shasta meets Aslan face to face in the dead of night and learns the true nature of his adventures. It was Aslan who seemed to be two lions chasing the riders together. It was also he who took the form of a cat to comfort Shasta at the tombs, frightened away the jackals and chased the two exhausted horses to the safety of the hermitage.

Like similar scenes in other Chronicles, Shasta's first encounter with Aslan is suffused with a sense of the numinous. Asked who he is, Aslan simply answers "*Myself*" three times, first in a voice low and deep so as to shake the earth, then in a voice clear and glad, then in a barely audible whisper that "seemed to come from all around you as if the leaves rustled with it." The thrice-repeated answer suggests the doctrine of the Trinity. The third answer is especially evocative: the soft whisper evokes the "still small voice" Elijah heard, and the allusion to rustling leaves recalls Christ's words about the wind blowing where it pleases, making a sound but not revealing the way of its coming or going (1 Kings 19:12; John 3:8).

When Aslan is transfigured, shining like the sun, Shasta dismounts and falls to his knees, feeling that "no-one ever saw anything more terrible or beautiful." Aslan's departure is described in terms so numinous as to be almost visionary: "Then instantly the pale brightness of the mist and the fiery brightness of the Lion rolled themselves together into a swirling glory and gathered themselves up and disappeared. [Shasta] was alone with the horse on a grassy hillside under a blue sky. And there were birds singing."

While the Chronicles often embody Otto's concept of the numinous, they also illustrate Edwyn Bevan's ideas about metaphors for portraying the Divine. Aslan is always the great lion in *The Magician's Nephew* and *The Lion, the Witch and the Wardrobe*. But he seems to appear in *The Horse and His Boy* as two nontalking beasts, Calormene lions, as a cat and finally as a kind of mountain lion. (In *The Voyage of the "Dawn Treader"* he will be incarnated in two other forms—an albatross who leads the ships out of dread darkness and a lamb who welcomes them as they near Aslan's country.) Though the portrayal of Aslan as a lion, king of beasts, is a brilliant master metaphor for Lewis's imaginative supposal, he seemed to feel as the Chronicles developed that one metaphor alone was not enough.

In *Symbolism and Belief* Bevan noted that the faith of the Hebrews, as recorded in the Old Testament, is one of the *least* anthropomorphic of ancient world religions. While most other religions usually visualized incarnated gods in human form, the Lord God of the Israelites appears as a burning bush, a pillar of cloud and fire, a voice out of the whirlwind and a still small voice. In his fiction as in his nonfiction Lewis seemed to believe that any one picture of the Deity should be balanced and supplemented with others in order to express more fully the myriad dimensions of God's nature.

Prince Caspian

The mystical elements in *Prince Caspian* do not emerge until more than halfway through the story. The four Pevensie children are called back to Narnia by the magic of Susan's horn, only to find that in the one year they were back on earth many centuries have passed in Narnia. Arriving amid the overgrown ruins of their old castle, Cair Paravel, Peter, Susan, Edmund and Lucy have to wend their way cross-country to Aslan's How, site of the Stone Table where Aslan was slain in *The Lion, the Witch and the Wardrobe.* There a band of Old Narnians, led by rightful heir to the throne, young Caspian, are waging a desperate rebellion against his usurping uncle Miraz. It is a time of apostasy, when even many dwarves and talking beasts no longer believe in Aslan.

As the Pevensies, led by the loyal dwarf Trumpkin, are trying to make their way across rugged terrain, Lucy sees Aslan on an uphill slope when the others are making their way down. She tries to persuade the others they are going the wrong way, but no one else saw anything out of the ordinary. In a magnanimous gesture Edmund takes Lucy at her word, even in the absence of other evidence. It is a poignant instance of spiritual healing: this same Edmund was the traitor in *The Lion, the Witch and the Wardrobe,* the one who pretended not to believe Lucy even though he had seen Narnia with his own eyes. By the end of that story, though, he had matured into a Narnian king known as Edmund the Just. In *Prince Caspian,* again a boy, he becomes Edmund the Trusting, believing where he cannot see.

Lucy and Edmund, however, are overruled by the others, and the group continues hiking downhill. That night, as they are camped out under the stars, Lucy awakes from a deep sleep, "feeling the voice she liked best in the world had been calling her name." (This scene echoes another numinous episode in Scripture, the calling of the young Samuel by name in the middle of the night [see 1 Samuel 3:1-10].) Lucy follows the voice and finds Aslan, shining in the moonlight, seemingly a great deal larger than she remembered. "You're bigger," she exclaims, to which Aslan replies, "That is because you are older, little one." He goes on to explain that he has not changed, but that "every year you grow, you will find me bigger."

In these few lines of dialogue Lewis encapsulates with elegant simplicity one of the most oft-repeated themes in the tradition of Christian mysticism. The modern inspirational writer J. B. Phillips proclaimed, "Your God is too small." Christian mystics might rephrase this as "Your capacity to experience God is too small." Almost two thousand years ago the apostle Paul wished for the Ephesians that they might gain the power to grasp the width and length and height and depth of Christ's love.

Three hundred years later Augustine prayed for God to enlarge his soul because it seemed too small for God to enter. The same yearning is eloquently expressed in Bernard of Clairvaux, Walter Hilton and George MacDonald. Mysticism scholar William R. Inge has summed up this recurring idea: "The world as it is, is the world as God sees it, not as we see it. Our vision is distorted, not so much by the limits of finitude, as by sin and ignorance. The more we raise ourselves in the scale of being, the more will our ideas about God and the world correspond to reality."

Lucy's encounter with Aslan is also intriguing because he warns her in advance that the others may not be able to see and hear him the way she does. Sure enough, Lucy discovers later that no one—not Peter or Susan or Edmund or the dwarf—can see the same Aslan who is so vividly present to her eyes and ears. But this time Lucy insists she will follow Aslan, even if she has to go alone. Again Edmund supports her and so the others follow, though rather halfheartedly. After a long time walking, Edmund sees Aslan's shadow, then the lion himself. Eventually, Peter can see him too and, finally, Susan. Of course, Aslan leads them along the path they had been seeking, so that they can join the others, eventually helping restore the young king to his rightful throne. As Peter Schakel has noted, this scene in *Prince Caspian* illustrates a recurring theme in Lewis: not the common idea that seeing is believing but the uncommon one that sometimes believing is seeing.

THE VOYAGE OF THE *DAWN TREADER*

Of the dozens of characters we meet in the Narnia Chronicles, the one whom Lewis himself described as a kind of mystic seems at first an unlikely candidate. It is Reepicheep, the chivalric mouse. In a letter to a girl named Anne, Lewis summarized *The Voyage of the "Dawn Treader"* as a story about "the spiritual life (especially in Reepicheep)." In another letter, this time to a group of children, Lewis explained that the valiant mouse is not an allegorical figure but that "anyone in our world who devotes his whole life to seeking Heaven will be *like* Reepicheep."

In many ways Reepicheep, with his elegant sword and flowery

speech, seems more a comic figure than an exemplar of "the spiritual life." But he is a knight on a quest, one who has been haunted all his days by words he first heard in his cradle from his nurse, a wood nymph:

> Where sky and water meet,
> Where the waves grow sweet,
> Doubt not, Reepicheep,
> To find all you seek,
> There is the Utter East.

In Lewis's fiction the things children learn from their nurse and the things they learn from a children's story or rhyme usually turn out to be true. Reepicheep says he has been under the spell of this rhyme all his life, and he intends to seek out the Utter East and, possibly, to reach Aslan's country. Obviously, the rhyme evokes in the noble mouse a kind of Sweet Desire, like the piercing pleasure the young Lewis felt on reading Longfellow's lines about Balder. If the young Lewis heard the call of "Northernness," Reepicheep might be said to be under the spell of "Easternness."

Reepicheep's quest to reach Aslan's country seems the Narnian equivalent of the Grail quest of Arthurian knights on earth. In medieval romances mere bravery or physical prowess is not enough to achieve the Grail; the quester must also have purity of soul, like the morally unblemished Galahad. Lewis told a friend, in fact, that some of the details associated with Aslan and his country—the luminescence, the mysterious yet delightful fragrances—were taken from Grail quest stories.

As critic Evan Gibson has observed, Reepicheep is the true Dawn Treader in this story. The ship nearly runs aground near the World's End, but Reepicheep casts away his sword and sails over the edge in his little boat. He vanishes from the sight of the others, but the narrator tells us he believes Reepicheep really did make it safely to Aslan's country (a fact confirmed in *The Last Battle*). In this respect Reepicheep resembles those like Elijah and Enoch in the Bible, who are "translated" directly into God's presence without having to suffer death.

As in the earlier Chronicles, Lucy Pevensie's experiences in *The Voyage of the "Dawn Treader"* often take on mystical overtones. The tale she reads "for the refreshment of the spirit" in the Magician's Book creates in her the same kind of *Sehnsucht* that Reepicheep felt about the Utter East. And the lesson Lucy must learn about not trying to repeat the experience recalls Ransom's insight on Perelandra of not clinging to pleasures that are only given once.

Lucy's mystical sensibility is even more strongly suggested by her response to Aslan on learning it is time for her to return to her own world: " 'It isn't Narnia, you know,' sobbed Lucy. 'It's *you*. We shan't meet *you* there. And how can we live, never meeting you?' " Once again Lewis uses a few simple words to underscore one of the most often-sounded themes in mystical literature: that the great gift to be sought is not health or wealth, escape from earthly troubles, or mansions in the sky. It is to be in perfect communion with the all-loving, all-good Almighty. As the fourteenth-century Flemish mystic John Ruysbroeck declared, "If God gave us all but himself, we would still be hungry." Catherine of Genoa sounded a similar note in the next century: "I desire not what comes from Thee, but only Thee." At about the same time Thomas à Kempis, whose *Imitation of Christ* (1426) is one of the books Lewis quoted most often in his letters, wrote in a notebook, "I would rather be in hell with Christ than to be in heaven without Him." But then he crossed out the words, deciding that being close to Christ is the very definition of heaven.

To Lucy's great comfort Aslan tells her that she can meet him in her own world under another name: "This was the very reason you were brought to Narnia, that by knowing me here for a little, you may know me better there." With these words Aslan the lion reveals himself more fully to Lucy. And Lewis the author reveals himself to his readers, reminding them again of his strategy in writing the Chronicles. The artist in him took simple delight in telling good stories and telling them well. But the spiritual mentor in him wanted to help readers steal past the "watchful dragons" of rote religion, so that they could be dazzled anew by the treasures within.

THE SILVER CHAIR

Near the end of *The Voyage of the "Dawn Treader,"* Reepicheep fulfills his quest to sail past the World's End toward Aslan's country. Early in *The Silver Chair* Lewis takes his readers to see Aslan's country for themselves. By its very nature this is a mystical place, the main setting in the story where characters can talk to Aslan face to face.

In earlier Chronicles Lewis had portrayed Aslan as ageless and luminescent—two of the qualities attributed to deity in most world mythologies, according to Edwyn Bevan. In this story Lewis highlights, may we say, the third quality noted by Bevan—height. When Eustace Scrubb and Jill Pole are carried from Experiment House on earth directly to Aslan's country, they soon find themselves at the edge of an unimaginably high precipice. From where they stand, the tiny, white specks they see far below are actually great, billowy clouds in the sky above Narnia. Eustace soon loses his balance trying to look out for Jill, and he goes sailing off to safety on the breath of Aslan. Jill is left to face the solemn lion alone, not at all feeling it a great privilege to come to Aslan's country without having died first.

As with so many other scenes in the Chronicles, this encounter with Aslan calls to mind numinous episodes in the Bible. Most importantly, it echoes Moses and the burning bush on Horeb, "the mountain of God" (Exodus 3:1). The Lord, who identifies himself as I AM, calls Moses for a specific task, to free the Israelites from bondage. Though she doesn't know it at first, Jill and Eustace have also been called for a mission, to free a Narnian prince from the bondage of a witch's enchantment. When Jill timidly asks the great lion if he is "Somebody," Aslan replies simply, "I am." He goes on to explain the signs Jill and Eustace will need in order to fulfill their quest, stressing their importance: "First, remember, remember, remember the Signs. Say them to yourself when you wake in the morning and when you lie down at night, and when you wake in the middle of the night." These words closely echo Moses' injunctions to his people to remember the law they have been given: "These commandments that I give you today are to be upon your hearts. . . . Talk about them when you sit at home and when you walk along the road, when you lie down and when you get up" (Deuteronomy 6:6-7).

Before sending Jill to begin her quest, Aslan also reminds her that the clarity of that moment will fade once she leaves the transcendent realm and enters into the world below: "Here on the mountain I have spoken to you clearly: I will not often do so down in Narnia. Here on the mountain the air is clear and your mind is clear; as you drop down into Narnia, the air will thicken. Take great care it does not confuse your mind." Aslan's warning turns out to be a prophecy, as Jill and Eustace neglect the first three signs in their mission to find and free the missing prince. However, through the help and good judgment of their companion, Puddleglum (plus a dream visit from Aslan), Jill and Eustace are able to fulfill their quest and restore Prince Rilian to his proper place.

Having completed their mission the children are carried back to what is called "the Mountain of Aslan," where they see the body of Rilian's father, Caspian, who has died of old age. Eustace weeps at the loss of his friend from the *Dawn Treader* voyage, and Jill weeps with him. Like Christ before the tomb of Lazarus, Aslan weeps as well, "great Lion-tears, each tear more precious than the earth would be if it was a single solid diamond." But he also provides a drop of blood from his paw, all that is needed to restore Caspian to life and youth. He reminds the children that he too had once died and come back to life, that drop of blood a reminder of his sacrifice. In Aslan's country, whether in this life or the next, all that was old is made new.

THE LAST BATTLE

The last of the Narnia stories provides some of the most depressing scenes in all the Chronicles, followed by some of the most glorious. The opening words of the book, "In the last days of Narnia," make it clear from the outset that this will be an account of the Narnian apocalypse.

Just as the creation of Narnia in *The Magician's Nephew* echoed the book of Genesis, its destruction in *The Last Battle* certainly calls to mind the book of Revelation. Shift the ape is a kind of Narnian anti-Christ, presenting a simple-minded donkey, covered in a lion's skin, as Aslan re-turned after a long absence. This new, angry Aslan is not at all like the Aslan of past ages. He allows living trees to be cut down, Narnians to be enslaved and Calormenes to enter as an occupying army. When the rightful Narnian ruler, King Tirian, protests all this as a horrible sham, he is knocked down by Calormene soldiers and taken prisoner.

Tied to a tree that night Tirian thinks about all the stories from the past when Aslan, with the help of children from another world, had come to the rescue of Narnia in its times of greatest need. "But it was all long ago," he thinks to himself sadly, "That sort of thing doesn't happen now." Nonetheless, he cries out in desperation, "Children! Children! Friends of Narnia! Quick. Come to me! Across the worlds I call you; I Tirian, King of Narnia, Lord of Cair Paravel, and Emperor of the Lone Islands!" At that moment, explains the narrator, Tirian is "plunged into a dream (if it was a dream) more vivid than any he had had in his life." He sees a vision of seven people around the table in some other world. Their leader identifies himself as Peter the high king, and he calls the others the seven friends of Narnia. Tirian can be seen but cannot speak, and soon the vision fades. But before long it is clear that his plea has been heard, as Eustace and Jill appear again in Narnia. They have come to play their part in what will become the Narnian apocalypse—with a false Aslan, believers led astray, great battles and finally the very dissolution of nature.

In the first several chapters *The Last Battle* is a "naturalistic" story, with no enchantments, passages between worlds or appearances by Aslan. It is Tirian's dream-vision that provides the first clue that once again "Aslan is on the move." In several of the Chronicles, Aslan appears in the guise of a dream to accomplish his work. In *The Horse and His Boy* Shasta thinks he must be dreaming when Aslan changes from cat to lion to scare away the jackals. In *Prince Caspian* he calls Lucy's name in the middle of the night to help the group get back on the right path. (She knows she is awake, though the others tell her later she must have been dreaming.) In *The Voyage of the "Dawn Treader"* Eustace's "undragoning" occurs in the form of a dream, and its setting is not the island but rather somewhere in Aslan's country—a mountaintop with a well of living water. And in *The Silver Chair* the lion appears to Jill Pole in a dream to help her understand the true meaning of the signs she has started to forget.

As is well known, dreams are often portrayed in the Bible as channels for divine communication—to Jacob, Joseph, Daniel, even to nonbelieving kings and pharaohs. Of course, this belief is much broader than Judeo-Christian tradition. There is very nearly a universal intuition that dreams convey truths hidden to the waking intellect. This can be found everywhere from classical myths and medieval allegories to modern therapies and self-help books. So Lewis was drawing on a very broad tradition in his use of revelatory dreams as signs of the numinous. But he seemed to have some special fascination for the idea, as it occurs so often in his fiction. In *Out of the Silent Planet* Ransom's dream of a walled garden marks his transition to a new plane of experience. In *Perelandra* his splendid mystical vision of the Great Dance is compared to a dream or trance. And in *That Hideous Strength* Jane Studdock discovers that her terrible nightmares are a form of second sight, that she has the power of "dreaming realities."

Though he generally discouraged an interest in "signs and wonders," Lewis did make the cryptic remark once that he had not seen visions, but he had dreamed dreams (see chap. seven, p. 160) It must be recalled, of course, that all those numinous dream scenes occur in Lewis's works of fiction. Nevertheless, the very pervasiveness of the pattern suggests that Lewis may have viewed the otherworld of dreams as a kind of looking glass, however dark and distorted, for catching glimpses of the Otherworld affirmed by faith.

The whole last third of *The Last Battle* is an imaginative portrayal of that other world, where Aslan rules over all, where death is no more and where the friends of Narnia from all generations may join together. On that eternal morning they begin an adventure that will last for all time and beyond time. There too, in the new Narnia, every mortal being's final destiny is revealed. Lewis depicts this not so much as Judgment Day as Acknowledgment Day. It is every person's response to Aslan's face, either unutterable joy or unutterable misery, that determines who will spend eternity in fellowship with him and who will be sent as far away as distance and darkness can separate them from his presence. Lewis's portrayal of final judgment in *The Last Battle* aptly illustrates his assertion in *The Great Divorce:* "There are only two kinds of people in the end: those who say to God, 'Thy will be done,' and those to whom God says, in the end, '*Thy* will be done.' "

The final chapters of *The Last Battle* might be seen as some of the most mystical passages to be found anywhere in Lewis's writings. But in another sense they are not mystical at all. Lewis once described mystics as those who receive "wonderful foretastes of the fruition of God vouchsafed to some in their earthly life." In this last of the Chronicles, Lewis imaginatively portrays not foretastes but tastes, not earthly life but the one that comes after. There are no temples in the heavenly city as described in the book of Revelation. And there will be no need for mysticism in an abiding place of eternal Presence, whether you call it the new Narnia or the new Jerusalem.

~ *Seven* ~

LEWIS'S CRITIQUE

OF MYSTICISM

*T*hough Lewis evinced a lifelong interest in mystical texts, he was not an uncritical admirer of mysticism in general. He said the anti-Christian philosophies of his generation contained a good deal of "spurious mysticism." And he complained about the "horrid Aphrodite mysticism" he found in some modern fiction. Even among the Christian mystics he most admired, Lewis sometimes found unbalanced theology or uncritical thinking. In *Perelandra* Lewis has his hero, Elwin Ransom, warn Edward Weston—too late—to be careful: "There are spirits and spirits, you know." In a larger context Lewis might want to warn his readers, "Be careful. There are mysticisms and mysticisms, you know."

MYSTICISM AS AN ECLECTIC WORLD RELIGION

Lewis certainly rejected the idea of mysticism as a kind of New Age world religion transcending all cultures and traditional theologies. He thought all religious traditions contain elements of truth but that Christianity offers the fullest and most perfect revelation of unseen realities. He noted that descriptions of mystical "departures" might well be similar in terms of the changes in consciousness mystics experience, but the important point is *where they arrive,* the content of their visionary intuitions. As he concluded, "The true religion gives value to its own mysticism; mysticism does not validate the religion in which it happens to occur."

As so often happened, Lewis anticipated a key issue that would become much more pronounced in the decades after he lived. In current mysticism studies there are two contrasting schools, the "perennialists" and the "constructivists." The earliest generation of modern scholars, many of whom Lewis read, stressed that mysticism constituted a "perennial philosophy," a system of core experiences and beliefs that did not vary all that much from mystic to mystic or culture to culture. These generally assumed that all mystics are encountering the same Absolute, however one may define it. The perennialists, who take their name from Aldous Huxley's *The Perennial Philosophy* (1944), included Huxley himself, as well as Rudolf Otto, Richard Bucke and more recently Alan Watts and W. T. Stace. One of the most popular contemporary voices for perennialism is Huston Smith, author of the bestselling *The World's Religions*. Smith believes that "the central insights of the perennial philosophy, which mystics know firsthand" may be summarized as follows: "First, reality is more unified than it appears; second, reality is better than it ordinarily seems to us; third, reality is more mysterious than it looks."

Despite the ongoing popularity of the perennialists, mysticism studies in recent years have been dominated by the constructivists, scholars who stress that beliefs and values are socially constructed, that no one can have an unmediated experience of the Absolute. Early forerunners of constructivism include William R. Inge and R. M. Jones, and more recently the case has been made by Steven Katz, Peter Moore and Ninian Smart. Constructivists charge perennialists with naiveté, saying no one can apprehend transcendental realities directly, without reference to prior beliefs and experiences. They also fault writers like Otto and Huxley for skewing their quotations and translations to make similarities between Eastern and Western mystical texts seem more striking than they actually are.

Contemporary mysticism scholar Robert K. C. Forman acknowledges constructivist criticisms of perennialism but suggests that constructivists may be overstressing differences between mystical texts the same way perennialists overstress similarities. The difference between perennialists and constructivists may ultimately be that of seeing the glass of mystical universals as half full or half empty.

However one lines up on this issue (Christian scholars seem about equally divided), it is clear that mysticism in and of itself does not offer a coherent religious worldview. As mentioned in chapter one (p. 32), Lewis considered it "nonsensical" to suppose that logically contradictory statements about God could be equally true. This is certainly an obstacle for those like Huston Smith who find an underlying unity in all the mystical traditions of the world. The Hindu sees our world, our bodies, as illusions to be transcended. The Christian sees them as broken vessels, groaning to be mended. The Buddhist sees an inert blankness at the center of things, a voiceless Void. The Christian sees a dazzling, holy but loving face, the "Face above all worlds." Only by emptying language and logic of all meaning can these opposites be reconciled under the rubric of mysticism. The contradictions are too fundamental to disappear with the agreeable thought that life is more mysterious, harmonious and unified than we suspect.

In its fullest sense, mysticism is not a method for discovering transcendental truths; it is a way of living. Mysticism is less about *seeing* than about *being*. Though the word *mystical* goes back to the early church, originally referring to hidden meanings in Scripture passages, the term *mysticism* did not appear until the late seventeenth century, after it became more a subject for scholars than a way of life. As Bernard McGinn has noted, Augustine, Francis of Assisi and Teresa of Ávila, however mystical-minded they may have been, did not view themselves as adherents of something called mysticism. Rather they considered themselves followers of Christ.

In this context Lewis's comments about the pantheism of his day apply equally well to the world mysticism of ours. For example, he warned about philosophies of life that demand no cost of discipleship, no denial of self. In *Miracles* he describes the god of pantheism as an Absolute who "does nothing, demands nothing. He is there if you wish for him, like a book on a shelf." The same might be said of a world mysticism, a philosophy that offers a glimpse into the heart of things without requiring one to examine one's own heart.

In her classic study *Mysticism* Evelyn Underhill stressed repeatedly that "transformation is the essence of mystical life," adding that the proper quest of the mystic is not "I want to know" but "I want to be." Contemporary authority Bernard McGinn makes the same point, arguing that in the Christian tradition mysticism focuses on transformation, not information. Lewis would surely agree, as he noted that God revealed himself to fallen humans not in order to satisfy their intellectual curiosity but to remake them into his image. Ultimately, the contemporary trend in world mysticism must be found wanting, both for its logical inconsistencies and for its empty promise of *gnōsis* without *kenōsis*, the gaining of knowledge without the losing of self.

MYSTICISM AND MAGIC

Where there is evidence of spiritual power, there will be those who are drawn to the power, regardless of the spirit. Shadowing Simon Peter is Simon the sorcerer, someone who thinks the gifts of the Spirit can be had for pieces of silver (Acts 8). Competing with the apostle Paul is a magician, Elymas, whom Paul calls "child of the devil" and strikes temporarily blind (Acts 13). It seems the more precious the gift, the more likely there will be counterfeits.

Lewis assumed this would be true of mystical gifts. He said that he would not be surprised to discover that the use of drugs or a "diabolical mysticism" could simulate mystical *sensations,* though they could not reproduce *content* of authentic mystical insight.

Lewis probably borrowed the term "diabolical mysticism" from William James, who used the phrase to describe certain types of insanity, calling it "a sort of religious mysticism turned upside down." James was fascinated by altered states of consciousness, and he experimented with psychoactive drugs, attended séances and studied the speech and behavior of the mentally ill. James noted that psychotics, like mystics, may experience voices or visions, and they often find hidden meanings in seemingly insignificant things. But he said these states of mind leave the subject with "desolations, not consolations," with meanings that are dreadful, not blissful, and "powers [that] are enemies to life." James concluded that there are regions of the mind where both "seraphs and snakes" may dwell, and so any reports of mystical encounters should be "sifted and tested . . . using empirical methods."

James's research into the paranormal sounds rather speculative and spooky by today's standards. He belonged to the Society for Psychical Research, founded in 1882, an organization that advocated empirical study of occult phenomena. For most of the nineteenth century the prestige and influence of science had been growing while that of traditional religion had been on the decline. In the closing decades of that century and the opening decades of the next, there was a kind of twilight period in which serious scientific minds wondered if "supernormal phenomena," as they called it—hypnotic trances, spirit mediums, Ouija boards, divining rods and so forth—could be studied using the methods of scientific research.

The young C. S. Lewis was extremely interested in this new, "scientific" approach to the paranormal. In the summer of 1917 he studied W. F. Barrett's *Psychical Research* (1911), Frederic W. H. Myers's *Science and a Future Life* (1893), a survey of paranormal phenomena, and Sir Oliver J. Lodge's *Raymond, or Life and Death* (1916), about attempts to communicate with the dead through spirit mediums.

Besides his interest in those who took a more scientific approach, Lewis in his adolescence was also drawn to literary figures who wrote about magic. (By *magic*, of course, Lewis did not mean entertainers who perform sleight-of-hand tricks. Rather he was referring to those who claim to have contact with the dead or to call on occult forces.) Lewis discovered Maurice Maeterlinck the same month he first read George MacDonald, not realizing the mystical elements he found in the two writers were almost opposite. Maeterlinck (1862-1947), the Belgian dramatist and essayist, is now remembered mainly for his symbolic children's fantasy *The Blue Bird*. But Maeterlinck's lesser-known plays were also imbued with occult overtones, and in his later years he wrote explicitly about his interest in spiritualism.

Besides Maeterlinck, Lewis in his teens was devouring the occult speculations of Irish poet William Butler Yeats. The whole world of séances, paranormal phenomena and occult traditions seemed at first look to offer Jack some middle ground between an arid atheism and an oppressive orthodoxy. Spiritualism seemed to offer many of the consolations of religion without its obligations. A person might take comfort in the possibility of life after death, the assurance that lost loved ones had survived in another world, without shouldering the burdens of orthodox belief or the guilt of repeated moral failure.

By his late teens, however, the young Lewis's interest in spiritualism had begun to fade. Lewis later felt he was protected from spiritual debauchery by his practical ignorance of magic, by childlike apprehensions about "bogies" and by an abiding instinct that this was not the road to his ultimate desire. In *Surprised by Joy* Lewis speculated that he might have ended up as a satanist or a madman if he had encountered someone during those vulnerable years who dabbled in the dark arts. Yet it did not take him long to realize that, even if he could have discovered the proper incantations, the secret formulation of circles, pentangles or other magic symbols used to call forth a spirit, it might be extremely interesting—if his nerves held up—but it had nothing to do with his real spiritual quest. Eventually he would dismiss his adolescent passion for the paranormal as a kind of "spiritual lust" and dismiss the occult as a painted impostor of the true joy.

Lewis's declining interest in magic turned to outright revulsion after a series of encounters during his undergraduate years at Oxford. First came two disappointing meetings with William Butler Yeats, the great Irish poet who was more than a little enthralled by matters occult. Lewis had been reading Yeats since he was twelve, and he felt no one spoke for Ireland the way Yeats did. Yet when Lewis got a chance to sit down and talk face to face with Yeats, he felt he had encountered not Yeats the celebrated poet but Yeats the dabbler in magic. Though his encounter was a memorable one, his lingering impression seems to have been that the celebrated author's creative energy was being squandered on credulous and self-indulgent speculation.

Lewis met several other spiritualists at Oxford and was struck by how "unspiritual" they were. Their quest to find evidence for human survival beyond the grave was not linked to any desire to find God or even to be reunited with lost loved ones; it was a simple, almost monomaniacal, will to surmount death.

If Jack's attraction to the occult was seriously dampened by his actual meetings with what he called "Magicians, Spiritualists, and the like," his interest was utterly extinguished by a harrowing experience in the spring of 1923. He later described the ordeal in *Surprised by Joy* as a time when he spent fourteen days and nights trying to minister to "a man who was going mad." (This was Mrs. Moore's brother, John Askins.) During that time Jack had to help "hold him while he kicked and wallowed on the floor, screaming out that devils were tearing him and that he was that moment falling down into Hell." Though he recognized that there were probably physical causes for this disorder, Lewis could not help but associate his friend's psychic disintegration with a longtime preoccupation with the occult, including spiritualism and Theosophy.

From 1923 onward Lewis would associate magic with a particularly sinister kind of escapism and a possible route to diabolism or dementia. In his book-length poem *Dymer* (1926), written before his return to Christianity, Lewis portrayed a magician, who looks very much like Yeats, trying to convince a young wanderer, Dymer, that he can recapture "Eden fields long lost by man" by drinking an opiate-like elixir. Though the magician himself is troubled by night terrors and seizures, he is deeply offended when Dymer refuses to join him in his sorcerer's orgy. When the young man tries to escape, the magician wounds him with a rifle shot.

For the adult Lewis the sin of magicians is not just that they dabble in forbidden arts. More seriously, they have succumbed to the serpent's oldest temptation, "Ye shall be as gods." *Magic* and *magician* are specialized terms in Lewis's vocabulary, both in his fiction and his nonfiction. Andrew Ketterley in *The Magician's Nephew* is typical—wanting to manipulate occult forces for his own gain, exempting himself from ordinary morality because of his "high and lonely destiny," and disregarding the sanctity of life, whether human or animal. Though he is essentially a comic character, Andrew's magic shares a great deal with a misguided sort of scientism Lewis found all too prevalent in the modern era.

Occasionally, Lewis allowed for certain kinds of "good magic." He considered the kind of "fairy" magic we find in Arthurian romances as basically innocent in contrast to the insidious Renaissance sorcery of spells, charms and secret symbols. Fairy magic is merely a storytelling device, while Faustian magic is an actual attempt to wield occult powers in the real world. We can see the distinction between these two kinds of magic early in *The Silver Chair.* Jill Pole, who has never been to Narnia, suggests to her friend Eustace Scrubb that they try to travel to that enchanted world by drawing a circle on the ground and reciting special incantations. Eustace, who is more experienced in the ways of Aslan, pronounces that approach "rather rot," explaining that you cannot compel the lordly lion to do your will but can only make a request. As Eustace's remark suggests, the other "good magic" in Lewis is that which derives from the power of God, such as the "Deep Magic" and "Deeper Magic" in *The Lion, the Witch and the Wardrobe.*

Apart from these few exceptions, though, the word *magic* in Lewis's books nearly always refers to sinister attempts to exert an illicit control over nature or other people. In *The Abolition of Man,* for example, Lewis warned that beyond the obvious practical benefits of modern scientific advance, there could emerge a kind of religious energy very much like the old occult arts:

There is something which unites magic and applied science while separating both from the "wisdom" of earlier ages. For the wise men of old the cardinal problem had been how to conform the soul to reality, and the solution had been knowledge, self-discipline, and virtue. For magic and applied science alike the problem is how to subdue reality to the wishes of men.

Here Lewis touches on one of the themes that was closest to his heart: learning to accept what is given and to conform our will to reality rather than insisting on our own way and trying to bend reality to our will. Apart from the intrinsic dangers of the occult, the practice of magic also suggests an underlying attitude of not accepting our creatureliness, of trying to escape the intractable vulnerability of being human. Lewis expresses this thought most succinctly in "The Inner Ring," where he observes, "It is the very mark of a perverse desire that it seeks what is not to be had."

Herein lies the great distinction between mysticism and magic. Mysticism seeks purity; magic seeks mastery. Mysticism seeks to eradicate self-will; magic seeks to indulge self-will. Henri Delacroix, one of the best-known French scholars on mysticism, declares that its defining trait is "suppression of egoistic selfhood." Magic, on the other hand, is unbridled egoism, an attempt to channel occult forces for one's own ends. Evelyn Underhill has stated the difference succinctly: "Mysticism wants to give; magic wants to get."

The classical word for sorcery is *theurgy*, "god work," similar to our word *metallurgy*. The term suggests a notion that God, or the gods, can be bent and shaped to our own ends, like a rod of red-hot iron. Of course, God does not make such bargains, but there are tales of other spirits who do. As Dr. Faust is said to have learned one midnight, the infernal smell in his room did not come from molten metal.

In addition to his ultimate repudiation of magic, Lewis's early encounter with the occult also contributed to his sense of ongoing spiritual warfare just beneath the surface of the workaday world. In *Mere Christianity* he reaffirmed the traditional belief in a personal devil, not a cartoonish figure with hooves and horns but a fallen angel whose rebellion continues to plague our planet. He did not view Satan as the opposite of God but rather the opposite of an archangel like Michael. In *The Problem of Pain* Lewis asserted that both God and the devil have the power to influence human thoughts directly, even in those who believe in neither God nor the devil.

Lewis's most "diabolically clever" book, the one that brought him international fame, was *The Screwtape Letters,* first published in 1942. In these letters from a senior devil, Screwtape, to an apprentice tempter, Wormwood, Lewis allows his readers to view the two devils as literary caricatures, personifications of all the foibles and follies that cause humans to stumble in their spiritual journey. But at the end of the book he invites us to consider his devils as something more than metaphors. When Wormwood's "patient" is killed in an air raid, dying as a Christian in a state of grace, Lewis pictures the young man experiencing a "sudden clearing of his eyes." In his final moments the young Christian sees that his temptations did not all come from his "lower" nature but from somewhere lower than that. At the same time, the dying man can see angels, realizing "that he had always known them," suddenly understanding a "dim consciousness of friends about him which had haunted his solitudes from infancy." Like many of Lewis's most popular books, *The Screwtape Letters* begins on a note of rational psychology and ends on a note of mystical theology.

However much Lewis felt haunted by early encounters with the occult, however much he believed in dark spirits in the world, he considered it a great mistake to dwell too much on these matters. As he advised in his preface to *The Screwtape Letters:*

> There are two equal and opposite errors into which our race can
> fall about the devils. One is to disbelieve in their existence. The
> other is to believe, and to feel an excessive and unhealthy interest
> in them. They themselves are equally pleased by both errors and
> hail a materialist and a magician with the same delight.

MYSTICISM AND MIND-ALTERING DRUGS

Another counterfeit mysticism identified by Lewis was the use of psychoactive drugs. Once again, Lewis was prescient; one of the names currently in use for psychedelic drugs is *mysticomimetics,* chemicals that *mimic* mystical consciousness. (Advocates of such drugs call them *entheogenics,* "god-containing," while critics call them *hallucinogens,* "hallucination-causing" or even *psychotoxins,* "mind-poison.")

Again the pioneer researcher in this field was the American philosopher and psychologist William James. Some of James's experiments on himself were almost comic failures. When he tried peyote, James reported severe vomiting for twenty-four hours, but no visions. When he ingested ethyl chloride and asked his assistants to take down his every word, they reported later that the insight he offered during his drug-altered state was "The whole world smells like ethyl chloride." James had more success when he inhaled nitrous oxide (laughing gas) to study its effects on his mental state. He did feel a kind of chemically induced transport, a sense of some secret harmony at the center of things. This experience gave him second thoughts about ordinary, rational awareness. James concluded that our normal, waking consciousness is "parted by the filmiest of screens" from other forms of consciousness, that our everyday sense of reality may be less absolute than is often supposed.

After James's early experiments with mind-altering drugs, the boundaries between research and recreation became increasingly blurred. One of the earliest to advocate psychedelics as an aid to mystical insight was Aldous Huxley in *The Doors of Perception* (1954), an account of his sensations under the influence of peyote. Huxley reported that in his altered state he saw "what Adam had seen on the morning of his creation—the miracle, moment by moment, of naked existence." After that exalted preamble Huxley's description of his actual trip on mescaline (the psychoactive ingredient in peyote) is rather pedestrian. There is a chair that seems not to be a chair and objects around the room that sparkle like jewels. In general, Huxley's account sounds less like mystical revelation than like a 1960s fraternity party. Oxford scholar R. C. Zaehner offered a withering critique of Huxley's book in *Mysticism Sacred and Profane* (1961), arguing that altered perceptions have little to do with an altered worldview, much less an altered or improved character. Zaehner asserted that at best drug-based experiences might lead to low-level nature mysticism, an enhanced appreciation of one's natural surroundings, but they have little to do with the tradition of the mystical way.

Despite such critiques, Huxley's book became a countercultural classic in the 1960s and 1970s, to be followed later by Carlos Castaneda, Timothy Leary and a legion of other mind-expansion gurus. In general, the work of that generation has not fared well. Castaneda's *The Teachings of Don Juan: A Yaqui Way of Knowledge* (1968) was eventually exposed as largely fictitious. His alleged spiritual guide Don Juan turned out to be less a shaman than a sham. Timothy Leary evolved over the years from a serious scientist into a comic cult figure. None of those who preached the spirituality of mind-expanding drugs established new religious institutions. And a few of them ended up as residents in existing institutions.

In general, contemporary scholars on mysticism have reiterated Lewis's original assertion that drugs may simulate mystical *sensations,* but they can't reproduce the *content* of authentic mystical insight. Georgia Harkness studied drug-induced mental states and concluded they are a mere shadow of true mystical experience. She observed that the effects of mind-altering substances were temporary and often harmful, and that if they had any long-term effect, it was a debilitating one, not an increase in serenity or sanctity. Stephen Katz stated flatly that people who take psychedelics do not "have mystical experiences. They have *drug* experiences. All you're doing when you're taking a drug is experiencing your own consciousness." Even Huston Smith, who is open to the idea of mind-altering drugs as "entheogenics," comments that mature mysticism should lead to altered *traits,* not just altered states: "If you think you are advancing toward unity with God or the absolute and are not growing in love and charity toward your fellow person, you're just deluding yourself." Surely, Lewis would agree on this last point; for it was one of his principal mentors who explained two thousand years ago that "if I

have the gift of prophecy and can fathom all mysteries and all knowledge
. . . but have not love, I am nothing" (1 Corinthians 13:2).

MISGUIDED MYSTICS

Clearly, Lewis had little use for the counterfeit mysticisms of magic or
mind-altering drugs. But even in reading what he considered authentic
Christian mystics, he always weighed and assessed what he read in the
light of theological orthodoxy, "what has been believed by all Christians
in all places at all times."

We can see this critically evaluative attitude in Lewis's response to
Julian of Norwich's *Revelations of Divine Love*. Julian is one of the mystics
Lewis turned to most often, and he quotes her at least a half a dozen
times in his books. But in one of her "showings," when she asks Christ
how all can be well when some are destined for eternal condemnation,
he replies that he has planned a "Grand Deed" that will put even the final
destinies of condemned souls aright. Julian was so overwhelmed by her
sense of divine love that she felt somehow there would be no one lost
beyond finding, no tears that could not be wiped away.

Lewis was fascinated by this idea, both in Julian and another of his
spiritual guides, George MacDonald. But ultimately he rejected universalism, however much it might assuage his sadness about souls eternally
banished from the presence of God. Lewis felt there were simply too
many references in the Gospels to some "final loss," teachings from
Christ himself about the sheep and the goats, the wise and foolish virgins
and so on. However much he may have been impressed by the visions
of saints like Julian and MacDonald, he felt they must ultimately stand
under the correction of biblical teaching and church creeds. Lewis recalled that even though Origen was one of the most influential of early
church fathers, his speculations about universalism were roundly condemned as heresy by later church councils. ✱

Lewis's own method for sifting and weighing the insights of mystics
is explained in *Mere Christianity*. There he notes that even someone who
has had an authentic encounter with the divine nature should not pre-

✱ THESE ARE PRECEDENT-BASED ARGUMENTS AGAINST
UNIVERSALISM. BUT LEWIS ALSO USES LOGIC
ABOUT FREE WILL NOT BEING FORCED TO BE WITH GOD.

sume to contradict traditional Christian beliefs. By analogy, Lewis says that someone who has gazed on the Atlantic Ocean has had a firsthand experience that is not shared by someone who has only studied a map. But the person with the map still has a clearer overall picture, since it is based on the collective experience of thousands of people who have seen, swam in and sailed all parts of the Atlantic, not just one who walked along one edge. And the person with a map can actually voyage across the ocean to visit far-off lands, not just stand looking out from the shore.

In this approach Lewis echoed Evelyn Underhill, who wrote that there should always be a dynamic interaction and balancing of mystical theology with natural and historical theology. Lewis may have even borrowed his metaphor of ocean voyagers needing a map from Underhill; she used a similar analogy in her classic work, *Mysticism*.

Lewis also emphasized that experience in general is not self-interpreting. Nor is its meaning always self-evident. He defined the term *experience* as "that part or result of any event which is presented to consciousness." Given this definition it is clear that someone may have an authentic experience without fully understanding the total event. For instance, a person may experience intense pain in the mouth—undeniable pain, not something imaginary or delusional. Yet a dentist, someone with professional training with the proper equipment, may understand the total event, a decaying tooth, better than the person experiencing the pain firsthand. Lewis said that in recounting his own conversion to faith, he could only tell the story as he experienced it, not the total process as known by God.

Besides excessive trust in our own spiritual intuitions, Lewis also warned about excessive concern for how "spiritual" our feelings are. Medieval Christians are sometimes accused of excessive otherworldliness. Lewis did not seem to share this concern. After all, he is the one who wrote:

If you read history you will find that Christians who did the most for the present world were just those who thought most of the next. . . . It is since Christians have largely ceased to think of the other world that they have become so ineffective in this. Aim at Heaven and you will get earth "thrown in": aim at earth and you will get neither.

But if Lewis did not consider "otherworldliness" to be a snare, he did warn about what we might call "inner-worldliness," trying to gauge the presence or absence of God based on our emotional states. We can see this syndrome in Bernard of Clairvaux, for example, in his sense of the coming and departing of Christ's presence within:

I confess then that the Word has visited me—indeed, very often. . . . He is living and full of energy, and as soon as he has entered me, has quickened my sleeping soul, and aroused and softened my heart, which was torpid and hard as stone. . . . But when the Word withdrew, all my spiritual powers and faculties began to droop and languish, as if the fire were taken from beneath a bubbling pot; and this to me is a sign of His departure. Then my soul must needs be sad and sorry, till He comes back and my heart again warms within me. For this to me is the sign that He has returned.

Bernard may have been enough of a mystical adept to know the difference between a special sense of Presence and a mere fluctuation of emotions. But Lewis often cautioned against relying too much on our feelings as a barometer of our spiritual state. In one letter he congratulated a recent convert and discussed her feelings of exultation at length:

It is quite right that you should feel that "something terrific" has happened to you. . . . Accept these sensations with thankfulness as birthday cards from God, but remember they are only greetings, not the real gift. I mean it is not the sensations that are the real thing. The real thing is the gift of the Holy Spirit which can't usually be—perhaps not ever—experienced as a sensation or emotion. The sensations are merely the response of your nervous system.

Don't depend on them. Otherwise when they go and you are once
more emotionally flat, you might think the real thing had gone too.
But it won't. It will be there when you can't feel it. [It] may even be
most operative when you feel it least.

In the same letter Lewis goes on to say that the first flush of excite-
ment is like the parent's push to begin a child's bicycle ride. He tells the
new Christian to expect "lots of dogged pedaling later on," but not to
be discouraged as that is when she will be building up her "spiritual
leg muscles."

When asked by another correspondent if he had a personal sense of
spiritual realities, Lewis replied, "'Does God seem real to me?' It varies:
just as other things I firmly believe in (my own death, the solar system)
feel more or less real at different times. I have dreamed dreams but not
seen visions: but I don't think that matters a hoot. And the saints say that
visions are unimportant."

Lewis took very much to heart Walter Hilton's advice that we should
not try to manufacture the proper "spiritual" feelings in prayer. Lewis
also commented favorably on fifteenth-century French mystic Francis de
Sales's beginning each of his meditations with the same instruction:
Mettez-vous en la présence de Dieu: "Put yourself in the presence of God."
Obviously, Lewis agreed with Francis that Christian meditation begins in
an act of the will, not in waiting for a devotional mood to descend.

Unlike scholars such as William Inge and Evelyn Underhill, Lewis did
not see mysticism as the norm for Christian spirituality but rather as a
special calling. He considered mystical sensibility to be a natural gift the
Spirit could use in one person the way he might use physical strength in
another. But Lewis felt it would be as much a mistake for every Christian
to seek to be a mystic as it would to take up fishing for a living because
that is what so many of the disciples did. He believed as well that a charwoman who does her work to the glory of God fulfills her vocation as
fully as someone who has taken up the contemplative life. To a correspondent who asked Lewis if he believed in the inner guidance of the

Holy Spirit, he replied that he did indeed believe the Spirit could guide decisions made with the intent of pleasing God. But he reminded her that the Spirit does not speak *only* within; he speaks as well through the Bible, church services, Christian books and discerning friends.

MYSTICS AND MYSTIFICATION

Though he sometimes spoke of God as "imageless" and "transcending discursive thought," Lewis also felt that that negative theology, describing the Absolute by what it is not, could be overstated. If our attempts to describe the divine nature are utterly futile, then we are left not with mysticism but with agnosticism.

For example, Meister Eckhart declared that "calling God good is like calling the sun black. He is beyond any attributes we might name." Lewis seems to have read very little Eckhart, and it may have been because of statements like this one. Lewis emphatically disagreed that the Absolute is beyond our sense of good and evil. In Lewis's mind we worship God not because he is the supreme being, but because he is supremely good. Seeming almost to refute Eckhart directly, Lewis argues that "the Divine 'goodness' differs from ours, but it is not sheerly different: it differs from ours not as black to white but as a perfect circle from a child's first attempt to draw a wheel." Lewis adds that even in its crude early attempts, the child understands what it is *trying* to imitate. Lewis would never allow that we worship the "mere power" of the Divine, which he called "the most blackguardly of superstitions." What we bow down before in God is right, not might. The key concept here is not God as Wholly Other but God as the Holy Other.

In *Miracles* Lewis critiques apophatic mysticism at more length, offering the witty analogy of a "mystical limpet, a sage among limpets" who has a rapturous vision of a human being. Using only negatives, he explains to his fellow mollusks that humans may be defined as beings with no shells, with nothing to attach them to rocks and who don't live in water. To the other limpets this description evokes nothing more than a being who has no shape, exists nowhere they can imagine and seems not to need nourishment. They may conclude that a human is "a famished jelly in a dimensionless void." They may also dismiss any positive depictions of humans as too crude and superstitious.

Though Lewis talked about God as transcending human reason and imagination, he did not use the word *unknowable*. God's own self-disclosures, culminating in the incarnation, changed all that. As Lewis explained it, "This is the humiliation of myth into fact, of God into Man: what was everywhere and always, imageless and ineffable, only to be glimpsed in dream and symbol and the acted poetry of ritual, becomes small, solid—no bigger than a man who can lie asleep in a rowing boat on the Lake of Galilee." For Lewis, the incarnation is what brings into balance mystical, natural and historical theology. Of Christian faith he says, "We have something like knowledge-by-acquaintance of the Person we believe in, however imperfect and intermittent it may be. We trust, not because 'a God' exists, but because *this* God exists." Despite the difficulties Lewis insisted that Christians travel past propositions and paradoxes toward a Person—someone good, loving and trustworthy, their "increasingly knowable Lord."

~ *Eight* ~

LEARNING FROM
THE MYSTICAL WAY

Though Lewis was clearly well versed in the tradition of Christian mysticism, he never wrote about it at any length. He referred to mysticism dozens of times in his books and letters, and knew contemporary scholarship on the subject. But he never set down his thoughts on mysticism in a separate essay or book chapter, leaving only tantalizing hints scattered throughout his writings. Perhaps he considered the subject too divisive or too easily misunderstood. Or perhaps he didn't feel qualified to speak authoritatively on the subject.

Yet there is no doubt Lewis's spiritual intuitions were greatly enriched by his reading of Christian mystics and their interpreters. If he didn't think every Christian should embark on the mystical way, he clearly believed that every Christian will be able to learn from it. Lewis once distinguished between *believing* a doctrine and *realizing* it. Christians may assent to a doctrinal truth without its having much effect on their daily mindset. But once that truth is realized, embraced by head and heart, intellect and imagination, its transformative powers are greatly enhanced. For all Christians, studying the mystical way may prove a valuable resource for *realizing* the very doctrines they have already affirmed.

RATIONAL FAITH AND MYSTICAL FAITH

Some Christians today feel mysticism belongs to a bygone era, that faith should be built on reason and objective evidence, not on metaphor or personal experience. But Lewis argued "there is no real conflict between the Rational and the Mystical." He thought apparent contradictions between direct experiences of God and rational theology simply reveal the difficulties of finite brains trying to encompass the infinite mind. For Lewis a paradox may simply be a problem with a missing dimension. He offered the parable of two-dimensional Flatlanders who argue continually about whether the world is finite or if it is endless and boundless. A sage or mystic in their midst would tell both sides they are right. The world is finite, but a Flatlander traveling on its surface will never reach an end or boundary. The sage can see that the world has three dimensions, not just two. It is a globe, something that cannot even be visualized in Flatlander terms.

Contradictions or paradoxes may thus arise from limited perspectives on both sides of a question. Ask a Bedouin to describe the world, and he might say it is mostly land with small dots of water. Ask a South Sea Islander and she might say it is mostly water with small dots of land. But someone looking down from a space station would see right away the reason for their opposing views. The desert dweller and island dweller are both right: they simply occupy different points on a globe with unevenly distributed land masses. In the same way Lewis argued that Christians must sometimes remind rationalists that there are certain undeniable truths that "escape discursive thought." But to those who flee "scientific dogmatism" in favor of a "spurious mysticism," believers should be prepared to explain that "Reason is always on the side of Christianity."

Lewis did not think contemporary Christians need necessarily consider themselves mystics. He noted, for example, that the mystical way is never mentioned in the New Testament. Yet what many would consider routine religious exercises, Lewis talked about as bridgeheads between our world and another. For example, he noted something very different happening in the life of a person following Christ from those who might call themselves followers of Plato or Marx. These last two may assent to the ideas of earlier thinkers and try to live by their systems of thought. But none seeks directly the aid of Plato or Marx. By contrast, followers of Christ in the act of prayer are having their hearts and minds enabled by the very person they desire to emulate.

Lewis also taught that "the Christian is called, not to individualism but to membership in the mystical body." He noted that "God communicates His presence" directly to those engaged in praise and adoration, that for many people " 'the fair beauty of the Lord' is revealed chiefly while they worship Him together." Lewis also urged Christians to frequently call to mind their ultimate goal: "I must keep alive in myself the desire for my true country, which I shall not find till after death."

PUTTING ON CHRIST

Lewis defined the basic Christian walk not in terms of striving after ethical ideals but in terms of mystical transformation. In *Mere Christianity* he explained succinctly that "every Christian is to become a little Christ." He added that "putting on Christ" is "not one among many jobs a Christian has to do; it is not a sort of special exercise for the top class. It is the whole of Christianity."

What does it mean to "put on Christ"? At the very least it means to put *off* the Adam within. As Lewis put it:

All day long, and all the days of our life, we are slipping, sliding, falling away—as if God were, to our present consciousness, a smooth inclined plane on which there is no resting. . . . The gravitation away from God, "the journey homeward to habitual self," must, we think, be a product of the Fall.

Like the first pair, we crave a godlike control over our environment and over others. We prefer knowledge and power, instruments for securing the mastery of self, over self-emptying love and vulnerability. We constantly reach out for the attribute of divinity that we can never have:

sovereignty. We make the same mistake our first parents made: We would be as gods. And thereby we forfeit two attributes of divine perfection that we could have had—abiding love and eternal life.

How is God to redeem his creatures who have taken a wrong turn, reaching out for the one attribute of deity we can never fully attain? He cannot simply exchange our badness for goodness, our selfness for godness. This would violate our free will and negate our essential being as images of his nature. He can only point us back to the right path, give us revelations from without (Spirit-guided teachings and stories) and within (the witness and work of the Spirit directly on human consciousness).

If the Spirit is to carry on this reclamation project, he must have as a template the profoundest, most terrible test of the good that ever was, the greatest ever temptation to abandon self-emptying love and reach out for the power and control we all desire. Jesus was God in the flesh. But he emptied himself of divine power and knowledge—so much so that he didn't know the time and date of his return. And it appears he was not absolutely sure whether he had to go through the crucifixion. In Gethsemane he asked several times, in his terrible anxiety and sadness, if there were any other way the cosmic drama of redemption could be accomplished. There was not, and he obediently drank of that cup.

If humans were to be guided back to their true source, there needed to be the ultimate test: the human who would cling to love in the worst possible extremity, who would not reach out for self-preservation or power or control. Jesus passed the early tests when Satan offered him respite from physical hunger, earthly rule and glory, a chance to prove that angels would come to his aid. But these were low hurdles compared to the Passion. When Peter asked him if it could be avoided, Jesus recognized that as a ploy of Satan. At Gethsemane he asked the same question again, but ultimately, Jesus submitted his will if there could be no other way.

And so he underwent physical torture, humiliation, a slow, painful death. He endured betrayal or abandonment by his friends, mockery by the soldiers and crowds. Ultimately, in some way we cannot understand,

Jesus endured the despair of feeling abandoned by the Father, of taking upon himself all the sufferings, all the mistakes, all the sins and blasphemies of all humans at all times. And he bore the weight, did not flinch from the task. He did not call down angels to his rescue; he did not call out imprecations on his torturers or his faithless followers. Love passed the test; goodness was not broken, even when embodied in frail flesh at its worst extremity.

Somehow this act of the obedient Son, emptied of power in suffering flesh, was mystically taken out of time back up into the timeless, into the nature of the Godhead, somewhere beyond the stars. Lewis described the incarnation as not just the great redemptive moment in human history but as a cosmic event. He portrayed God coming down to earth in order to draw earthly things up into heaven:

> Sleep, sweat, footsore weariness, frustration, pain, doubt, and death, are, from before all worlds, known by God from within. The pure light walks the earth; the darkness, received into the heart of Deity, is there swallowed up. Where, except in uncreated light, can darkness be drowned?

Perhaps the atonement was also a work of vicarious empowerment. As the Spirit guides human spirits, the indwelling Infinite knows exactly what is being asked of every human heart. The Spirit, who is the same being as the Son, knows, with sighs that cannot be spoken, the profoundest possible test any human has ever faced. He can show all humans that their worst sufferings are known, their worst temptations can be overcome.

All human journeys are either back to God or away from him, falling further and further into self—pride and unloving and self-exile. We are all called on, as Lewis puts it, to "tread Adam's dance backward." We must unlearn the mistake of the first Adam and by God's grace imitate the second, innocent Adam. We must cease to reach for the godlike knowledge and power that were never ours, *could* never be ours, and reach instead for the godlike attributes we are more than welcome to—

eternal being and eternal loving. As Lewis puts it, "The whole purpose for which we exist is to be taken into the life of God."

We start by expanding the circle of what we value and cherish—from ourselves to our family to our tribe to all humanity to all creation. We can see this progressive revelation, the widening circle of value, as the Old Testament unfolds. And the whole journey is summarized by Jesus in his command to keep the whole law by loving God and loving our neighbors.

Of course, both these commands can seem daunting to souls still aching from our Eden exile. It may be more a discipline at first than habit of mind. But as the Spirit's inflowing energy becomes more available to seasoned travelers, his grace and love to us flow out to others as grace and love from us to them. It is not two different things: it is just the mirror, polished to perfection at great cost, reflecting a Light that will outlast the stars.

APPENDIX

A Brief Timeline of Christian Mystics

Clement of Alexandria (c. 150-c. 215). First to adapt the language of the Hellenistic mystery religions to a Christian understanding of the spiritual life.

Origen (c. 185-c. 254). Clement of Alexandria's pupil.

Plotinus (c. 205-270). The Neo-Platonic philosopher who influenced Augustine, Pseudo-Dionysius and later Christian mystics.

Augustine (354-430). Bishop of Hippo.

Pseudo-Dionysius the Areopagite (c. 475-525).

Benedict (c. 480-c. 550). Founder of Monte Cassino and Benedictine Order.

Maximus the Confessor (c. 580-662).

John Climacus (c. 570-c. 649).

Symeon the New Theologian (949-1022).

Bernard of Clairvaux (1090-1153).

Hugh of St. Victor, Paris (d. 1142).

Hildegard of Bingen (1098-1179). Called "the Sibyl of the Rhine."

Elizabeth of Schonau (1138-1165).

Richard of St. Victor, Paris (d. c. 1173).

Francis of Assisi (1182-1226). Founder of Franciscan Order.

Elizabeth of Hungary (1207-1231).

Mechthild of Magdeburg (c. 1210-c. 1280). Author of *The Flowing Light of the Godhead*. Possible model for the Eve-like character of Matilda in Dante's *Purgatorio*.

Bonaventure (c. 1217-1274). Author of *The Journey to God*.

Thomas Aquinas (c. 1225-1274). Author of *Summa Theologia*.

Angela of Foligno (c. 1248-1309).

Meister (Johannes) Eckhart (c. 1260-1327).

Dante Alighieri (1265-1321). Author of *The Divine Comedy*, a poem profoundly infused with the spirit of medieval Christian mysticism.

The Mirror of Simple Souls. Anonymous treatise written in the late thirteenth century.

Margery Kempe. Author of *Contemplations* in late thirteenth-century England.

John Ruysbroeck (1293-1381).

Gregory of Palamas (c. 1296-1359).

Richard Rolle of Hampole (c. 1300-1349).

Bridget of Sweden (c. 1303-1373).

Rulman Merswin (c. 1310-1382). Author of *The Book of the Nine Rocks*.

Julian of Norwich (c. 1342-c.1423). Author of *Revelations of Divine Love*.

Catherine of Siena (1347-1380).

Theologia Germanica. Written by "a man from Frankfurt" about 1350.

The Cloud of Unknowing. Anonymous late fourteenth-century treatise written in England.

Thomas à Kempis (c. 1380-1471). Author of the *Imitation of Christ*.

Walter Hilton (d. c. 1396). Author of *The Scale of Perfection*.

Nicholas of Cusa (1401-1464).

Catherine of Genoa (1447-1510).

Ignatius Loyola (1491-1556). Founder of the Society of Jesus (Jesuits) and author of the *Spiritual Exercises*.

Teresa of Ávila (1515-1582). Author of *The Interior Castle*.

John of the Cross (1542-1591). Author of *The Ascent of Mount Carmel* and *The Dark Night of the Soul*.

Francis de Sales (1567-1622). Cofounder of the Order of the Visitation.

Jacob Boehme (1575-1624). Author of *Aurora* and *The Signature of All Things.*

Brother Lawrence (c. 1605-1691). Author of *The Practice of the Presence of God.*

Blaise Pascal (1623-1662). Author of *Pensées.*

George Fox (1624-1691). Founder of the Society of Friends (Quakers).

Thomas Traherne (c. 1636-1674). Author of *Centuries of Meditations.*

William Law (1686-1761). Author of *A Serious Call* and *An Appeal to All Who Doubt.*

NOTES

Introduction: The Overlooked Lewis

Page 11   "Most Christians": Walter Hooper, "C. S. Lewis: Literary Chameleon," in *Behind the Veil of Familiarity: C. S. Lewis (1898-1998)*, ed. Margarita Carretero González and Encarnación Hidalgo Tenorio (Bern: Peter Lang, 2001), p. 25.

Page 11   *Practicing the Presence of God:* Title of a book about Brother Lawrence.

Page 11   "Perhaps some very good people": *Letters to Children,* p. 45.

Page 12   "Into the region of awe": *Surprised by Joy,* p. 221.

Page 12   "A boundary had been crossed": *That Hideous Strength,* pp. 318-19.

Page 14   "The morbid logician seeks": G. K. Chesterton, *Orthodoxy,* chap. 2.

Chapter 1: The Mystique of Mysticism

Page 15   "A reverential insensibility": Huxley, *Door of Perception,* p. x.

Page 15   God speaking to God: A phrase that occurs in several mystical writers. Lewis uses it in *Letters to Malcolm,* p. 68.

Page 17   James's definition of mysticism: James, *Varieties,* pp. 380-81; 408.

C. S. Lewis first read *The Varieties of Religious Experience* when he was in his mid-twenties, pronouncing it a "capital book." Even though these were years when Lewis considered himself an atheist, he seems to have read James's book with great care, reading it all one Thursday afternoon and evening in 1922 and saying he found the section on mysticism the most interesting part. The following Sunday morning, young Lewis reported in his journal that he woke up feeling miserable and depressed and was even a bit weepy. It is only speculation, of course, but I wonder if reading of all those accounts of finding a higher harmony may have contributed to this mood (see *All My Road Before Me*, pp. 49-51). Even though he considered himself a settled skeptic during these years, reading James may have been what Lewis would later call "the scent of a flower we have not found, the echo of a tune we have not heard, news from a country we have never yet visited" (*Weight of Glory*, p. 5).

Page 17   "Mystical states wield no authority": James, *Varieties*, p. 428.

Page 17   Mystical experiences do not necessarily supply new ideas: Jones, *Flowering of Mysticism*, p. 215.

Page 18   "The direct intuition": Underhill, *Mystics*, p. 9.

Page 18   "Every human soul has a latent capacity": Ibid., p. 11.

Page 18   "This happened to them": Ibid., pp. 12-13.

Page 18   "Not solitary beacons": Ibid., *Mystics*, p. 53.

Page 18   "The experience of coming into immediate relation": Inge, *Christian Mysticism*, p. v.

Page 18   "Seek as we have sought": Ibid., p. vii.

Page 19   "Direct experience of God": *Letters of C. S. Lewis*, p. 408.

Page 19   "There is no reasoning in it": Ibid.

Page 19   "If humans are incapable": Quoted in Alister E. McGrath, *Christian Theology: An Introduction* (Oxford: Blackwell, 1997), p. 162.

Page 19   "Truthful antithesis": *All My Road*, p. 301.

Page 20   "I was caught up to Thee": Augustine, *Confessions*, bk. 8, chap. 17, quoted in Underhill, *Mystics*, p. 63.

Page 20   "Oh Sion, thou city sole and single": Quoted in Otto, *Idea of the Holy*, p. 35.

Page 21   Pascal's "Night of Fire": O'Connell, *Blaise Pascal*, pp. 95-96.

Pages 21-22   "I remember that night": James, *Varieties*, pp. 66-67.

Page 22   Rufus Jones's own mystical experience: Jones, *Flowering of Mysticism*, p. 253; Harkness, *Mysticism*, p. 21.

Page 23   "Recovering the depth-life of the soul": Jones, *Flowering of Mysticism*, p. 6.

Page 23   "But we cannot insist too strongly": Inge, *Christian Mysticism*, p. viii.

Pages 23-24   Mystics who considered visions peripheral: Graef, *Story of Mysticism*, pp. 152, 205.

Page 25   "As a man feeleth God in himself": Quoted in "The Literary Impact of the Authorised Version," *Selected Literary Essays*, p. 132.

Page 25   "More is done for God": Quoted in Graef, *Story of Mysticism*, pp. 167-68.

Pages 25-26   "Even if one were in a rapture": quoted in Jones, *Flowering of Mysti-cism*, pp. 62-63.

Page 26   "Prince of Mystics": Baumgardt, *Great Western Mystics*, p. 21.

Page 26   "To give our Lord perfect service": Graef, *Story of Mysticism*, pp. 167-68.

Page 26   Mystical elements in Wesley, Nightingale, Mother Teresa: *Joy Wesley's Awakening*, pp. 61-66; Cook, *Life of Florence*, p. 42; Fraser, "Newly Released Letters," p. 1.

Page 26   "Psycho-physical elements": Underhill, *Mysticism*, p. vii.

Page 26   "Concrete, richly living yet unchanging": Ibid., p. viii.

Pages 26-27   "But some have every right": Inge, *Christian Mysticism*, pp. 17, 18.

Page 27   "Mystical experience is simply": Gimello, "Mysticism and Meditation," p. 62.

Page 27   Sources of mystics' visions: Graef, *Story of Mysticism*, p. 200; Forman, *Mysticism, Mind*, p. 2.

Page 27   "Science studies Nature": "Religion and Science," *God in the Dock*, p. 73.

Page 27-28   "Surely we cannot take": Chesterton, *William Blake*, pp. 73-74.

Page 29   "It is assumed": Chesterton, *All Things Considered*, p. 155.

Page 29   "All the facts, but not the meaning": "Transposition," *Weight of Glory*, p. 28.

Page 30   "Induce upon themselves": Ibid., p. 28.

Page 30   "Religion is only psychological": Ibid., p. 29.

Page 30   "Great Christian books": "On the Reading of Old Books," *God in the Dock*, pp. 204-5.

Page 30   "If Jacob had seen the unutterable": *Collected Letters* 2, p. 40.

Page 30   "Soul mysticism" and "God mysticism": Otto, *Mysticism*, p. 142.

Page 31   History of science versus history of mysticism: Baumgardt, *Great Western Mystics*, p. 12.

Page 31   Underhill on Trinity and incarnation: Underhill, *Mysticism*, pp. 107-8.

Page 32   "Clear that we are not pronouncing": "Christian Apologetics," *God in the Dock*, p. 102.

Page 32   "Nonsensical": Ibid.

Page 32   "Departures are all alike": *Letters to Malcolm*, p. 65.

Page 32   "Not at all on its being mystical": Ibid.

Page 32   "The true religion gives value": Ibid.

Chapter 2: Mystical Elements in Lewis's Life

Page 33   "People of the foothills": *Letters to Malcolm*, p. 63.

Page 33   Lewis radiated a spiritual sense: *They Stand Together*, p. 316.

Page 34   Habitual sense of yearning: Otto, *Idea of the Holy,* pp. 31-38.

Page 34   "All [my] life an unattainable ecstasy": *Problem of Pain,* p. 136.

Page 34   "Spiritual experiences as pure and momentous": Ibid., p. 67.

Page 34   "Cool, dewy, fresh": *Surprised by Joy,* p. 7.

Page 34   Always "over there": Unpublished autobiographical fragment 5. Available at the Marion E. Wade Center, Wheaton, Illinois.

Page 35   "Northernness": *Surprised by Joy,* p. 17.

Page 36   "Ludicrous burdens": Ibid., p. 62.

Page 36   "If only someone had read to me": Ibid.

Page 37   You should not get "too fearful": Hilton, *Scale of Perfection,* p. 105.

Page 37   Even if you fail in prayer a hundred times: Ibid., p. 106.

Page 37   "Great Christian books": "On the Reading of Old Books," *God in the Dock,* p. 204.

Page 38   "Nearly all that I loved": *Surprised by Joy,* p. 170.

Page 38   "Great literary experience": *They Stand Together,* p. 92.

Page 39   "Spiritual healing, of being washed": Ibid., p. 389.

Page 39   "Crossed a great frontier": *George MacDonald: An Anthology,* p. 25.

Page 39   "A sort of cool, morning innocence": Ibid., p. 26.

Page 39   "Did nothing to my intellect": Ibid.

Page 39   "The quality which had enchanted me": Ibid., pp. 26-27.

Page 39   "Mystic and natural symbolist": *Allegory of Love,* p. 232.

Page 40   "An inner harmony": Hein, *Harmony Within,* p. 7.

Page 40   "MacDonald felt deeply": Ibid., p. 30.

Page 41   "Penchant for mystical philosophy": *They Stand Together,* p. 97.

Page 41   "The beaten track, the approved road": *Surprised by Joy,* p. 203.

Page 41   "The Enemy": Ibid., p. 60.

Page 42   "The fuller splendor": Ibid., p. 210.

Page 42   "Terrible things are happening to me": *Letters of C. S. Lewis,* pp. 283-84.

Page 42   "Holding something at bay": *Surprised by Joy,* p. 224.

Page 43   "To open the door": Ibid.

Page 43   "The most dejected and reluctant convert": Ibid., pp. 228-29.

Page 43   "About the biggest shaking up I've got from a book": *They Stand Together,* p. 328.

Page 43-44   "It's not like a book at all": Ibid.

Page 44   "What on God's earth": Quoted in Hein, *Harmony Within,* p. 6.

Page 44   "Innumerable instances of physical law": Quoted in Ibid., p. 46.

Page 44-45   Jack's view of nature was "essentially mystical": Sayer, *Jack,* p. 148.

Page 45   "The world before the Fall": *Letters of C. S. Lewis,* p. 308.

Page 45   "Makes the Resurrection seem almost *natural*": *Collected Letters* 2, p. 377.

Page 45	"The whole business of life": Ibid., pp. 177-78.
Page 45	"He is pure Light": *They Stand Together,* p. 463.
Page 45	"Translation of it into non-spiritual terms": *Mere Christianity,* p. 139.

In speculating about "signatures" of the divine nature in the material world, Lewis is following a long tradition going back to the Bible and St. Augustine. Medieval mystics especially were drawn to images of the Trinity in the physical realm. Of all the recent developments in the natural sciences, I believe there are two that might have most fascinated the medieval mind:

1. Space and time feel to us like very different things. We measure one with a ruler, the other with a clock. But space-time is actually one thing, the fabric of the physical universe. In the spatial dimensions we can move both ways (up-down, left-right, forward-back). In time we can move only one way, into the future. Yet modern physics has shown that the two are ineluctably interwoven. It takes four coordinates to determine a person's location, three in space, one in time. Space and time are actually space-time, a three-in-one field in which all matter and energy exist.

2. The proton, nucleus of the simplest atom, hydrogen, and building block of all elements, is actually three quarks (two "up" quarks and one "down" quark) spinning around each other at nearly the speed of light. No one knows what forces hold the quarks together in this three-as-one configuration. Physicists whimsically call these unitive forces *gluons,* the "glue" of the nucleus. Perhaps they could just as well call them "colossions," after Colossians 1:17: "He is before all things, and in him all things hold together."

Page 46	"There have been times": *Problem of Pain,* p. 133.
Page 46	"The secret signature of each soul": Ibid., pp. 133-34.
Page 46	"First Fair": *English Literature,* p. 10. Lewis may have borrowed this name for God from Evelyn Underhill.
Page 47	"Wild and mystical": Sayer, *Jack,* p. 176.
Page 47	Eliot considers Williams a saint: Humphrey Carpenter, *The Inklings* (Boston: Houghton Mifflin, 1979), p. 107.
Page 47	"He makes our everyday world much more exciting": Ibid., p. 97.
Page 47	"The most precious moments to Jack": Sayer, *Jack,* p. 192.
Page 48	"Our Lord suffers": *Letters of C. S. Lewis,* p. 412.
Page 49	Lewis wondered if God welcomed souls: Unpublished letter to Vera Mathews Gebbert, March 27, 1951.
Page 49	"No event has so corroborated my faith": C. S. Lewis, ed., *Essays Pre-*

sented to Charles Williams (Grand Rapids: Eerdmans, 1966), p. xiv.

Page 49   Joy's special place in Lewis's heart: Sayer, *Jack,* p. 177.

Page 49   "Masculine virtues": *A Grief Observed,* p. 39.

Page 49   Joy's vision like a burning bush: Lyle Dorsett, *And God Came In* (New York: Macmillan, 1983), p. 1.

Page 49   "Haunted all one morning": *A Grief Observed,* p. 39.

Page 50   Lewis wondered if substitution was valid: Hooper, *Companion and Guide,* pp. 84-85.

Page 50   "Wonderful recovery Joy made": Ibid., p. 95.

Page 51   "Beyond hope, her greatest, lifelong, this-worldly desire": Ibid.

Page 51   Hooper's account of Lewis's vision: Hooper, "C. S. Lewis: The Man," pp. 27-28.

Page 51   Otto on Christianity as historical faith: Otto, *Idea of the Holy,* p. 62.

Chapter 3: Christian Mysticism as Lewis Knew It

Page 54   "Big with God": *Letters to Malcolm,* p. 75.

Page 54   "Here is the holy ground": Ibid., p. 82.

Page 54   "Every common bush was afire": Quoted in Underhill, *Mysticism,* p. 254.

Page 54   Incidents that will speak most fully: "The Literary Impact of the Authorised Version," *Selected Literary Essays,* p. 143.

Pages 54-55 "The stillness in which mystics approach": *Miracles,* p. 95.

Page 55   "The ultimate Peace is silent": Ibid., pp. 95-96.

            While writing about the literary qualities of the Authorized (King James) Version of the Bible, Lewis also had Elijah in mind. First, Lewis offers this sentence for the reader's inspection: "After the cocktail, a soup—but the soup was not very nice—and after the soup a small, cold pie." Then he quotes a KJV verse with the exact same prose rhythm: "After the earthquake, a fire; but the Lord was not in the fire: and after the fire a still, small voice (I Kings xix.12)." Lewis's point, obviously, is that the power of this verse comes from its numinous content, not from its literary cadences (*English Literature,* p. 214).

Page 55   Mystical description of God based on Isaiah 6: *Problem of Pain,* pp. 141-42.

Page 55   Ramandu scene: *The Voyage of the "Dawn Treader,"* pp. 176-80.

Page 55   Psalms appear more often: Underhill, *Mystics of the Church,* p. 34.

Page 56   "Ego dormio": Moynihan, "Sleep," p. 40.

Page 56   Underhill's interpretation of Jesus' words to Paul: Underhill, *Mystics of the Church,* pp. 37-38.

Page 56	"If Stephen had not prayed": quoted in Graef, *Story of Mysticism*, p. 50.
Page 57	Some scholars believe: Ibid., p. 37.
Page 58	"*Grace,* for Paul, was no theological abstraction": Underhill, *Mystics of the Church*, p. 48.
Page 58	"God speaks not only for us little ones": *Letters of C. S. Lewis*, p. 434.
Page 58	"One of the most important passages": McGinn, *Foundations of Mysticism*, p. 71.
Page 58	"He who has seen the Perfect": Underhill, *Mysticism*, p. 90.
Page 58	"A Christian is to Christ": "Christianity and Literature," *Christian Reflections*, p. 6.
Page 58	"Native luminosity": *Four Loves*, p. 180.
Page 59	"Goodness as a mirror": *Mere Christianity*, pp. 130-31.
Page 59	"The faces of friends": *Letters to Malcolm*, p. 124.
Page 60	"Martyrdom always remains": *Problem of Pain*, p. 90.
Page 60	"Nevertheless I am not for this reason a disciple": Graef, *Story of Mysticism*, p. 54.
Page 60	"Christ's pure bread": Ibid., p. 57.
Page 60	"My birth is imminent": Ibid., p. 56.
Page 60	"Eighty-six years have I been his servant": Ibid., p. 57.
Page 61	"I saw the glory of the Lord": Ibid., p. 58.
Page 61	"Now it is I who suffer": Ibid., p. 60.
Page 61	Story of Perpetua and Felicita: Williams, *Descent of the Dove,* p. 28; Hoagland, Book of Saints, pp. 57-58.
Page 63	"Be not afraid": Augustine, *Confessions*, bk. 8, chap. 11.
Page 63	"Take and read": Ibid., bk. 8, chap. 12.
Page 64	"Then with our affections burning": Ibid., bk. 9, chap. 10.
Page 65	"The Prince of Mystics": Butler, *Western Mysticism*, p. 24.
Page 65	"Dialog of the deaf": McGinn, *Foundations of Mysticism*, p. 230.
Page 65	"I entered into my inmost parts": Augustine, *Confessions*, bk. 7, chap. 10, quoted in McGinn, *Foundations of Mysticism*, p. 233.
Page 65	"Seeing God invisibly": McGinn, *Foundations of Mysticism*, p. 232.
Page 65	"The presence of the face of God": Ibid., p. 240.
Page 65	Types of visions: Ibid., p. 254.
Page 66	"Great saint and a great thinker": *Four Loves*, p. 167.
Page 66	Lewis recommended Augustine's *Confessions: Letters of C. S. Lewis*, p. 497.
Page 66	"Late have I loved you, O Beauty": Augustine, *Confessions*, bk. 10, chap. 27. Referred to in *Letters to Malcolm*, p. 28.
Page 66	"The house of my soul": Quoted in part in "Christianity and Litera-

	ture," *Christian Reflections,* p. 9; this phrasing is from Chadwick.
Pages 66-67	"I saw well": *Till We Have Faces,* p. 294.
Page 67	"And where was I": Augustine *Confessions,* bk 5, chap. 2; Augustine, *The Confessions of Saint Augustine,* trans. Rex Warner (New York: New American Library, 1963), p. 91.
Page 67	"Thou hast made us for thyself": *Four Loves,* p. 189.
Page 67	"The imperishable beauty": Graef, *Story of Mysticism,* p. 96.
Page 68	"O Trinity": Quoted in Egan, *Anthology,* pp. 96-97. Arranged as poetry by the translator because of all the verbal repetitions. The use of the word *mysticism* in the English translation is an anachronism.
Page 68	C. S. Lewis discussed Pseudo-Dionysius: *Discarded Image,* pp. 70-74.
Page 68	"The burning and undimensioned depth": *Miracles,* pp. 160-61.
Page 69	"The conscience of all Europe": Egan, *Anthology,* p. 166.
Page 69	"That the great God": Quoted in Graef, p. 138.
Page 69	"Communion of wills": Quoted in Ibid., p. 139.
Pages 69-70	"So when the Bridegroom, the Word": Quoted in Egan, *Anthology,* p 175.
Page 70	"O how rare is the hour": Quoted in Graef, *Story of Mysticism,* p. 140.
Page 70	"[The visit to my soul] terrifies not": Quoted in Ibid., pp. 140-41.
Page 71	"Great spiritual writers": *Discarded Image,* p. 18.
Page 71	French study: *Allegory of Love,* p. 21.
Page 71	"One of the many endearing": James, *Saint Bernard,* p. 153. Most of the books from Lewis's personal library have been collected at the Marion E. Wade Center, Wheaton College, Wheaton, Illinois.
Page 71	"Shining examples of human holiness": *They Stand Together,* p. 503
Page 71	"Brother Ass": *Four Loves,* p. 143.
Page 71	Lewis signed his own letters "Bro. Ass": *Collected Letters* 2, pp. 556, 567, 812, 961.

This was a running joke in Lewis's letters to Sister Penelope, an Anglican nun at the convent of the Community of Saint Mary the Virgin at Wantage. Reporting that his talks on Christianity to Royal Air Force personnel seemed like a complete failure, Lewis took comfort from the passage in Numbers 22, where Balaam's ass spoke on behalf of the Lord. Lewis signed later letters to Penelope "Bro. Ass," but the pen name gradually took on Franciscan connotations, in reference to Lewis's bodily self. When Penelope reported that she was feeling worn out, he reminded her that she too needed to take care of "Bro. Ass" (*Collected Letters* 2, p. 962).

Page 72	"The most blessed result": *Letters to Malcolm,* p. 82.
Page 72	"Great Christian books": *God in the Dock,* p. 204.

Page 72   More elegant writers: *English Literature*, p. 181.

Page 73   "All shall be well"; "our true Mother": Walsh, *Literary Legacy*, pp. 292, 298.

Pages 73-74   Lewis's response to Julian: *Collected Letters* 2, pp. 369-70.

Page 74   Lewis concluded his sermon "Miracles": *God in the Dock*, p. 37.

Page 74   "All shall be well": *God in the Dock*, p. 124; *Christian Reflections*, p. 122.

Page 74   "Wonderful foretastes": *Four Loves*, p. 175.

Page 74   "I, and me and mine": Winkworth, *Theologia*, p. 21.

Page 75   "Hell is nothing but self-will": Ibid., p. 138.

Page 75   Lewis cites the *Theologia*: *Christian Reflections*, p. 17.

Page 75   Lewis recommended *Theologia Germanica*: *They Stand Together*, p. 561.

Page 75   Natural self's horror at submitting: *Problem of Pain*, p. 77.

Page 75   Loving God simply for his goodness: Ibid., p. 140.

Page 75   Texts by Roman Catholic mystics: Teresa: Unpublished letter to Sheldon Van Auken; Brother Lawrence: *They Stand Together*, pp. 351, 541; Pascal: *Problem of Pain*, p. 1; *God in the Dock*, p. 203; *Letters to Malcolm*, p. 11.

Page 77   "To enjoy what you have not": St. John of the Cross, *Collected Works of St. John of the Cross*, p. 67.

Page 77   The sixteenth-century Spanish word *escura*: Underhill, *Mysticism*, p. 354.

Page 77   "Dark night of the flesh": *Christian Reflections*, p. 125.

Page 78   We take the mysticism of saints seriously: *Letters to Malcolm*, pp. 64-65.

Page 78   "It is saints, not common people": Ibid., p. 44.

Page 78   "I do not call myself the Damning One": Egan, *Anthology*, p. 467.

Page 79   "Elevated and united to God": Ibid., *Anthology*, p. 479.

Page 79   "Honey-eyed and floral" quality: *God in the Dock*, p. 203.

Page 79   "Beauty of holiness": *English Literature*, p. 181.

Page 79   True Christian renunciation: "Two Ways with the Self," *God in the Dock*, p. 193.

Page 79   "Green, dewy chapter": *Letters to Malcolm*, p. 98.

Page 80   Nicholas of Cusa et al.: Nicholas of Cusa: *Poems*, p. 70; Thomas à Kempis: *Discarded Image*, p. 18; Loyola: *Letters to Malcolm*, p. 84; *Cloud of Unknowing*: *Discarded Image*, p. 70; Weil: *Letters to Malcolm*, p. 30.

Chapter 4: The Mystical Way in the Space Trilogy

Page 81   Adam and Eve as first mystics: *Problem of Pain*, pp. 65-66.

Page 81   Inner divisions of mind and body: Ibid., pp. 68-69.
Page 81   "Spoiled species": Ibid., p. 73.
Page 81   "Tread Adam's dance backwards": Ibid., p. 89.
Page 81   "Retrace our long journey from Paradise": Ibid., p. 89.
Page 82   Communion: Harkness, *Mysticism*, pp. 23-24.
Page 82   Presence of God: McGinn, *Foundations of Mysticism*, p. xvii.
Page 83   "One of the high lights of my literary life": *Collected Letters* 2, p. 459.
Page 83   Praised by someone of her stature: Ibid., pp. 234-35.
Page 83   "Other-world of the spirit": "On Stories," *Of Other Worlds*, p. 12.
Pages 83-84 Outline of the mystic way: Underhill, *Mysticism*, pp. 91, 169-70.
Page 85   "The Pedestrian": *Out of the Silent Planet*, p. 7.
Page 85   Ransom's appearance: Ibid.
Page 85   Looked more like a gardener: Como, *"C. S. Lewis at the Breakfast Table,"* pp. 53, 71, 93.
Page 85   Ransom's traits: *Out of the Silent Planet*, pp. 17, 27, 35, 37.
Page 85   Not meant to be a self-portrait: Glover, *C. S. Lewis*, p. 77.
Page 86   "Delirious terror or an ecstasy of joy": *Out of the Silent Planet*, p. 23.
Page 86   "Planets of unbelievable majesty": Ibid., p. 31.
Page 86   "Spiritual cause": Ibid., p. 32.
Page 86   "Empyrean ocean of radiance": Ibid., p. 32.
Page 86   "Older thinkers had been wiser": Ibid., p. 32.
Page 87   "In these hours the world seems charged": Underhill, *Mysticism*, p. 22.
Page 87   "Ransom's *enfance*": Green and Hooper, *C. S. Lewis*, p. 179.
Page 87   "Frightened child": *Out of the Silent Planet*, p. 25.
Page 87   "One besetting sin is anxiety": Walsh, *Literary Legacy*, p. 86.
Page 87   "Twitching feelers": *Out of the Silent Planet*, p. 35.
Page 87   "Monstrous union": Ibid.
Page 87   Landscape of surpassing beauty: Ibid., p. 42.
Page 88   Further conversations: Ibid., pp. 67-68.
Page 88   Christian symbols in *Out of the Silent Planet*: Glover, *C. S. Lewis*, p. 79.
Page 88   "What God might be supposed to have done": *Letters of C. S. Lewis*, p. 261.
Page 89   Does not see an eldil: *Out of the Silent Planet*, p. 71.
Page 89   "Imagination and the dance of sunlight": Ibid., p. 79.
Page 89   "Footsteps of light": Ibid., p. 109.
Page 89   "Silvery noises in the air": Ibid., p. 109.
Page 89   Angels have bodies made of ether: *Letters to Children*, p. 73.
Page 89   "Any amount of theology can be smuggled": *Letters of C. S. Lewis*, p. 322.
Page 89   "A day in my life that has shaped me": *Out of the Silent Planet*, p. 75.

Pages 89-90   Hyoi's mystical encounter: Ibid.

Page 90   Ransom's renewed anxieties: Ibid., pp. 86-88, 93, 97.

Page 90   Pfifltrigg: Ibid., pp. 112-13.

Page 90   "Safe monster": Flieger, "Sound of Silence," p. 52.

Page 90   "You are guilty of no evil": *Out of the Silent Planet*, p. 142.

Page 91   "Quite astonishing pleasure": *Perelandra*, p. 35.

Page 91   "The laugh, rather than the roar, of heaven": Ibid., p. 37.

Page 91   "Cord of longing": Ibid., pp. 102-3.

Page 91   "Sharp, sweet, wild, and holy": Ibid., p. 103.

Page 92   Two colors of body: Ibid., p. 55.

Page 92   A variety of psychological models: See, for example, Corbin Scott
              Carnell, "Ransom in C. S. Lewis' *Perelandra* as Hero in Transforma-
              tion: Notes Toward a Jungian Reading of the Novel," *Studies in the Lit-
              erary Imagination* 14, no. 2 (1981): 67-71; Lee D. Rossi, *The Politics of
              Fantasy: C. S. Lewis and J. R. R. Tolkien* (Ann Arbor, Mich.: UMI Re-
              search Press, 1984), p. 39.

Page 92   Accepted change and mortality: *Out of the Silent Planet*, pp. 72-75.

Page 93   Whole new kind of pleasure: *Perelandra*, p. 42.

Page 93   "An oratorio or a mystical meditation": Ibid., p. 49.

Page 93   Demanding to hear the same symphony twice in one day: Ibid., p. 43.

Page 93   Multiply the enchantment tenfold: Ibid., p. 48.

Page 93   "Itch to have things over again": Ibid.

Page 93   "A defence against chance": Ibid.

Page 93   But, Ransom asks, what if she had clung: Ibid., p. 68.

Page 93   We would make the fruit we found taste insipid: Ibid., p. 69.

Page 94   "Clung longer": Ibid., p. 83.

Page 94   "Yes. It has ceased and still he clings": Ibid.

Page 95   "With my mother's death": *Surprised by Joy*, p. 21.

Page 95   "I thought I was carried": *Perelandra*, p. 69.

Page 95   "Outward eyes": Ibid., p. 62.

Page 95   She also knows about the incarnation on Earth: Ibid.

Page 95   Maleldil has told her: Ibid., pp. 61, 75, 80.

Page 95   Sense of fullness in the air: Ibid., p. 61.

Pages 95-96   "A sort of splendour" Ibid., p. 72.

Page 96   When he tries to assert his own will: Ibid.

Page 96   "There are spirits and spirits you know": Ibid., p. 93.

Page 96   "I call that Force into me": Ibid., p. 96.

Page 96   Ransom's fears: Ibid., p. 130.

Page 97   A sense of Presence in the darkness: Ibid., p. 140.

Page 97   "Prostrated in a hush of fear and love": Ibid., pp. 140-41.
Page 97   "Inner silence": Ibid., p. 140.
Page 97   "Silence and the darkness": Ibid., p. 141.
Page 97   "With his ridiculous piebald body": Ibid.
Page 97   "Man of straw": Ibid., p. 142.
Page 97   "Managed corpse": Ibid., p. 122.
Page 97   "Degrade spiritual warfare": Ibid., p. 143.
Page 97   Distinction between myth and fact: Ibid., p. 144.
Page 97   "All this he had thought before": Ibid.
Page 98   "The terrible silence": Ibid.
Page 98   "Mechanized corpse": Ibid., p. 129.
Page 98   "Voice in the night": Ibid., pp. 147-48.
Page 98   Ransom can hear a voice: Ibid., p. 147.
Page 98   Piebaldness has largely faded away: Ibid., p. 151.
Page 98   "Get out of my brain. It isn't yours, I tell you!": Ibid., p. 181.
Page 99   Weston's egocentric voice: Ibid., pp. 96, 129-30, 165-71.
Page 99   "Heart of the whole book": Collected Letters 1, p. 560.
Page 100   "Santo monte": Dante, Purgatorio, canto 28, line 12.
Page 100   "The privilege, the dreadful joy": Underhill, Mysticism, p. 201.
Page 100   "Stain the white radiance of eternity": Ibid., p. 204.
Page 100   Soul as ragged urchin: Letters to Malcolm, p. 108.
Page 100   "In reality every real Christian": Letters of C. S. Lewis, p. 467.
Page 100   "Holy mountain": Perelandra, p. 196.
Page 100   Angel with a flaming sword: Ibid., p. 193.
Page 101   "Not a process, but a state": Ibid., p. 192.
Page 101   "Trans-mortal journey": Ibid.
Page 101   Descriptions of seraphim: Dante, Purgatorio, canto 29; Letters to an
             American Lady, p. 12.
Page 101   Primum mobile as a dancing girl: Studies in Medieval and Renaissance
             Literature, p. 60.
Page 101   "Are to be conceived": Ibid.
Page 101   "Serious business of heaven": Letters to Malcolm, p. 93.
Page 102   "(All of Him dwells) within the seed": Perelandra, p. 215.
Page 102   "Where Maleldil is": Ibid., p. 216.
Page 102   "We should have in our minds": Ibid., p. 218.
Page 102   "God is in all, and all is in God": Quoted in Inge, Christian Mysticism,
             p. 28.
Page 102   "As small as a grain of mustard seed": Quoted in Underhill, Mysticism,
             pp. 100-101.

Page 102   "Unplumbed Abyss of God": Ibid., p. 229.
Page 102   "The part of him which could reason": *Perelandra,* p. 219.
Page 102   "Zenith of complexity": Ibid.
Page 102   "Simplicity beyond all comprehension": Ibid.
Page 102   "A quietness, a privacy, and a freshness": Ibid.
Page 103   "The splendour": Ibid., p. 222.
Page 103   "Peaceful joy, enhanced powers": Underhill, *Mysticism,* pp. 169-70.
Page 103   Active engagement: Ibid., pp. 173, 195.
Page 103   "The great native Christian mystic": *That Hideous Strength,* p. 114.
Page 104   "The holy one": Lindskoog, "Links," p. 3.
Page 104   "Other religions say": Streeter and Appasamy, *Message of Sadhu,* pp. 8, 61, 80. Lewis's underlined volume of this book is available at the Wade Collection in Wheaton, Illinois.
Page 104   Portrayal of Ransom: *That Hideous Strength,* p. 143.
Page 105   Isle of Avalon: Ibid., pp. 268, 274.
Page 105   Great goal of every mystic: Underhill, *Mysticism,* p. 171.

Chapter 5: Finding Words to Explore the Mind of God
Page 107   "It's too *definite* for language": *Perelandra,* p. 33.
Page 107   "If God exists at all": *Miracles,* p. 93.
Page 107   James's analogy of the iron rod: James, *Varieties,* p. 56.
Page 108   "Why prate of God?": Quoted in Huxley, *Perennial Philosophy,* p. 125.
Page 108   "The soul can never attain the heights": St. John of the Cross *Ascent of Mount Carmel,* bk. 1, pt. 2, chap. 15.
Page 108   "In one instant what words cannot express": Quoted in Underhill, *Mysticism,* p. 182.
Page 108   "Incomprehensible"; "inexpressible, unthinkable": *Miracles,* p. 77.
Page 108   OT references: Job 36:26; Psalm 145:3; Isaiah 55:8-9.
Page 108   NT references: 1 Corinthians 9:1; Ephesians 3:3-5; 2 Corinthians 9:15; Ephesians 3:8; Philippians 4:7; 1 Timothy 3:16; 1 Corinthians 13:12-13.
Page 109   Otto's definition of the term *numinous:* Otto, *Idea of the Holy,* p. 10.
Page 110   "Unimaginably or Insupportably Other": *Letters to Malcolm,* p. 13.
Page 110   "God is a self-subsistent Being": Moynihan, "I Sleep," p. 39.
Page 110   "Into the region of awe": *Surprised by Joy,* p. 221.
Pages 110-11 Mechthild's hymn: *The United Methodist Hymnal* (2001), p. 104.
Page 112   Modern theologians substituting new metaphors: "Is Theology Poetry?" *Screwtape Proposes a Toast,* p. 53.
Page 112   Anecdote of the girl envisioning God as tapioca: *Miracles,* p. 75.

Page 113   "It comes to us from writers": "Weight of Glory," *Weight of Glory,* p. 6.

Page 113   Any metaphor needs to be balanced: Ibid., p. 8; *Miracles,* p. 72; *Mere Christianity,* p. 151; *Four Loves,* p. 174.

Page 113   "This is also Thou": *Letters to Malcolm,* p. 74; see also Charles Williams, *War in Heaven* (Grand Rapids: Eerdmans, 1976), p. 146.

Page 113   Scene in Revelation: Discussed in *Letters to Malcolm,* p. 13.

Page 113   "What soul ever perished": Ibid., p. 22.

Page 113   Master's metaphors versus pupil's metaphors: "Bluspels," *Selected Literary Essays,* p. 255.

Page 113   Atomic model versus particles and waves: This example is adapted from two separate passages in Lewis: *Problem of Pain,* p. 74; *Letters of C. S. Lewis,* p. 433.

Page 114   Better to accept the Bible metaphors: *Mere Christianity,* p. 151.

Page 114   "Grammatically, the things we say": *Miracles,* p. 94.

Page 115   "The numinous is luminous": Bevan, *Symbolism,* p. 130.

Page 115   Bevan on different types of metaphors: Ibid., pp. 11-12, 28, 251-54.

Page 116   "If one drop of what I feel": Quoted in Otto, *Idea of the Holy,* p. 38.

Page 116   "The Love that made the worlds": *Problem of Pain,* p. 35.

Page 116   "A corollary of divine goodness": Ibid., p. 46.

Page 116   "The Father delights in His Son": *Mere Christianity,* p. 151.

Page 116   "Begetting love" and "love begotten": "Poison," *Christian Reflections,* p. 80.

Page 117   God's love is not a wavering passion: *Miracles,* p. 95.

Page 117   "Love may forgive all infirmities": *Problem of Pain,* p. 34.

Page 117   God is "easy to please, but hard to satisfy": *Mere Christianity,* p. 172.

Page 117   "Unappeasable distaste": *Problem of Pain,* p. 46.

Page 118   "I saw no wrath": Happold, *Mysticism,* p. 293.

Page 118   Lewis pronounced *Appeal* one of the best: *Letters of C. S. Lewis,* pp. 289-90.

Pages 118-19   "God darts no more anger": Law, *Writings,* p. 55.

Page 119   "God is never annoyed with anybody": Comer, *Wisdom,* p. 52.

Page 119   "Grandfather in heaven": *Problem of Pain,* p. 28.

Page 119   A person can forgive: *Letters to Malcolm,* p. 96.

Page 119   Accept the *purport* of the analogy: Ibid., pp. 51-52.

Page 120   Short-term anxiety about hell versus long-term longing: Ibid., p. 76; the phrase "the Mighty Beauty" is from Underhill, *Mystics of the Church,* p. 13.

Page 120   "Divine sorrow at the heart of things": Underhill, *Mysticism,* p. 178.

Page 120   "Love and sorrow": Ibid., p. 194.

Page 120   "World-sadness": Flanagan, *Hildegard of Bingen,* p. 72.

Page 120   George MacDonald on Christ's Passion: *Problem of Pain,* p. 140.

Page 121   Lewis recalls Christ's lament: For a book-length treatment of this topic, see Terence E. Fretheim's *The Suffering of God* (1984). Fretheim argues that Old Testament pictures of God are often dismissed too lightly. He says that "metaphors matter" because they are "reality depicting," going on to demonstrate that the Old Testament portrays a God who suffers *because of* his people's rejection of him who suffers *with* his people and who suffers *for* his people.

Page 121   Lewis also notes: *Letters of C. S. Lewis,* p. 412.

Page 121   "An anguish, an alienation": *Letters to Malcolm,* p. 44.

Page 121   God as tragic Creator: Ibid., p. 91.

In past centuries speculation such as this might be labeled "patri-passionism," the heresy that the Father suffered along with his incarnate Son. But the historic objection to this belief was that it blurred the distinction between two persons of the Trinity, Father and Son. So long as the doctrine of the Trinity is affirmed, there is a great deal of contemporary interest, especially in the Eastern Orthodox Church, in the image of God as cosufferer with his people. See Alister E. McGrath, *Christian Theology: An Introduction* (Oxford: Blackwell, 1997), pp. 250-54.

Page 122   "For the tawny face": *Magician's Nephew,* p. 142.

Page 122   "The serious business of heaven": *Letters to Malcolm,* p. 93.

Page 123   "It seems impossible": "Weight of Glory," *Weight of Glory,* p. 10.

Chapter 6: Mystical Elements in the Narnia Chronicles

Page 125   "A many-islanded sea of poetry and myth": *Surprised by Joy,* p. 170.

Page 125   "A glib and shallow rationalism": Ibid.

Pages 125-26 "Pure moonshine": "Sometimes Fairy Stories," *Of Other Worlds,* p. 36.

Page 126   "Everything began": Ibid.

Page 126   "An imaginary world": Ibid., p. 37.

Page 126   "Steal past those watchful dragons": Ibid.

Page 126   "You are mistaken": *Letters to Children,* pp. 44-45.

Page 127   Lewis's letter about the order of reading: Ibid., p. 68.

Page 127   "Do not dare not to dare": *Horse and His Boy,* p. 193.

Page 128   "Come in by the gold gates": *Magician's Nephew,* p. 157.

Page 128   "Shall have a long bright morning": Ibid., p. 142.

Page 128   "Principle of Vicariousness": *Miracles,* pp. 122-23.

Page 129   "It [is] the rule": *Collected Letters* 2, p. 953.

Page 129   Examples of the numinous: *Problem of Pain,* p. 6.

Page 130   Reactions to the name Aslan: *Lion, the Witch and the Wardrobe,* p. 64.

Page 130   "But as for Aslan himself": Ibid., p. 123.

Page 131   Pauline Baynes didn't think of Christ: Hooper, *Companion and Guide,* p. 625.

Page 131   Theological questions about the atonement: Taliaferro, "A Narnian Theory," pp. 78-79.

Page 131   "You must not confuse": *Collected Letters* 2, p. 914.

Page 132   Not understanding how the atonement works: *Mere Christianity,* pp. 59-60.

Page 132   "May have done": *Problem of Pain,* p. 74.

Page 132   "Some kind of 'inter-animation' ": Ibid., p. 75.

Page 132   "Strong magic": *Letters to Malcolm,* p. 103.

Page 132   "Can anything be done": *Lion, the Witch and the Wardrobe,* p. 124.

Page 133   "Seemed to come from all around": *Horse and His Boy,* p. 159.

Pages 133-34   Aslan's meeting with Shasta: Ibid., p. 160.

Page 134   Hebrew faith as less anthropomorphic: Bevan, *Symbolism,* p. 20.

Page 135   "Feeling the voice she liked best": *Prince Caspian,* p. 132.

Page 135   "You're bigger": Ibid., p. 136.

Page 136   "The world as it is": Inge, *Christian Mysticism,* p. 24.

Page 136   Believing is seeing: Peter Schakel, *Reading with the Heart: The Way into Narnia* (Grand Rapids: Eerdmans, 1979), p. 41.

Page 136   "The spiritual life": Hooper, *Companion and Guide,* p. 426.

Page 136   "Anyone in our world" *Letters to Children,* p. 45.

Page 137   "Where sky and water meet": *Voyage of the "Dawn Treader,"* p. 16.

Page 137   Borrowings from Grail quest stories: Walter Hooper, *Past Watchful Dragons* (New York: Collier Books, 1979), p. 95.

Page 137   Reepicheep is the true Dawn Treader: Evan Gibson, *C. S. Lewis: Spinner of Tales* (Grand Rapids: Eerdmans, 1980), p. 172.

Page 138   "For the refreshment of the spirit": *Voyage of the "Dawn Treader,"* p. 133.

Page 138   "It isn't Narnia, you know": Ibid., p. 215.

Page 138   "If God gave us all but himself": Underhill, *Mysticism,* p. 265.

Page 138   "I desire not what comes from Thee": Ibid., p. 248.

Page 138   Thomas à Kempis anecdote: Inge, *Christian Mysticism,* p. 9.

Page 138   "This was the very reason": *Voyage of the "Dawn Treader,"* p. 216.

Page 139   Aslan replies simply, "I am": *Silver Chair,* p. 19.

Page 139   "First, remember": Ibid., p. 21.

Page 140   "Here on the mountain": Ibid.

Page 140   "The Mountain of Aslan": Ibid., p. 211.

Page 140   "Great Lion-tears": Ibid.

Page 141   "But it was all long ago": *Last Battle*, pp. 40-41.

Page 141   "Children! Children!": Ibid., p. 42.

Page 141   "Plunged into a dream": Ibid.

Page 142   "Dreaming realities": *That Hideous Strength*, p. 65.

Page 143   "There are only two kinds": *Great Divorce*, p. 72.

Page 143   "Wonderful foretastes": *Four Loves*, p. 175.

Chapter 7: Lewis's Critique of Mysticism

Page 145   "Spurious mysticism": *Collected Letters* 2, p. 189; "horrid Aphrodite
              mysticism": Ibid., p. 875. Lewis was referring to the later romances of
              E. R. Eddison. Lewis also called modernist aestheticism as "mystical"
              but "amoral" ("Christianity and Literature," *Christian Reflections*, p.
              10) and associated pantheism with the outmoded ideas of "Pagan
              mystics" (*Problem of Pain*, p. 139).

Page 145   "There are spirits and spirits, you know": *Perelandra*, p. 93.

Pages 145-46 "The true religion gives value": *Letters to Malcolm*, p. 65.

Page 146   "First, reality is more unified": Quoted in Horgan, *Rational Mysticism*,
              p. 18.

Pages 146-47 Perennialists versus constructivists: See Forman, *Mysticism, Mind*, pp.
              31-33.

Page 147   "Nonsensical": "Christian Apologetics," *God in the Dock*, p. 102.

Page 147   "Face above all worlds": *Perelandra*, p. 111.

Page 147   Origins of words *mystical, mysticism*: McGinn, *Foundations of Mysti-
              cism*, pp. xvi, 12.

Page 147   Christian mystics were followers of Christ: Ibid., p. xvi.

Pages 147-48 God of pantheism "does nothing": *Miracles*, p. 96.

Page 148   "Transformation is the essence": Underhill, *Mysticism*, p. 272.

Page 148   "I want to know": Ibid., p. 150.

Page 148   Transformation, not information: McGinn, *Foundations of Mysticism*,
              p. xvi.

Page 148   God revealed himself: "Dogma and the Universe," *God in the Dock*, p.
              43.

Page 148   "Diabolical mysticism": *Letters to Malcolm*, p. 65.

Page 148   "Diabolical mysticism": James, *Varieties*, p. 426.

Page 148   "A sort of religious mysticism": Ibid.

Page 148   Altered states of consciousness: Ibid., p. 388.

Page 149   "Desolations, not consolations"; "powers [that] are enemies to life";

event: *Collected Letters* 2, pp. 928-29.

Pages 158-59 "If you read history": *Mere Christianity,* p. 118.

Page 159   "I confess then": Bernard of Clairvaux, *Canticles* 74, quoted in Under-
                    hill, *Mystics of the Church,* pp. 86-87.

Pages 159-60 "It is quite right": *Letters of C. S. Lewis,* pp. 421-22.

Page 160   "Does God seem real to me?": Ibid., p. 432.

Page 160   "Put yourself in the presence": *Letters to Malcolm,* p. 78.

Page 160   Lewis considered mystical sensibility a natural gift: *Collected Letters* 2,
                    p. 201.

Page 160   Charwoman pursuing a vocation: "Christianity and Culture," *Chris-
                    tian Reflections,* p. 24.

Page 161   Spirit does not speak *only* within: *Letters of C. S. Lewis,* p. 423.

Page 161   "Calling God good": Baumgardt, *Great Western Mystics,* p. 44.

Page 161   "The Divine 'goodness' differs from ours": *Problem of Pain,* p. 27.

Page 161   "Mere power": *Miracles,* p. 94.

Pages 161-62 Parable of mystical limpet: Ibid., pp. 91-92.

Page 162   "This is the humiliation of myth into fact": "Is Theology Poetry,"
                    Screwtape Proposes a Toast, p. 51.

Page 162   "We have something like": "On Obstinacy in Belief," *Screwtape Pro-
                    poses a Toast,* p. 70.

Page 162   "Increasingly knowable Lord": Ibid., p. 74.

Chapter 8: Learning from the Mystical Way

Page 163   Believing a doctrine versus realizing it: *Collected Letters* 2, p. 495.

Page 164   "There is no real conflict": Ibid., p. 189.

Page 164   Parable of Flatlanders: Ibid., pp. 369-70; see also "Bluspels," in *Se-
                    lected Literary Essays,* pp. 253-54.

Page 164   "Escape discursive thought": *Collected Letters* 2, p. 189.

Page 164   "Scientific dogmatism" versus "spurious mysticism": Ibid.

Page 164   "Reason is always on the side of Christianity": Ibid.

Page 164   Mystical way is never mentioned in the NT: Ibid., p. 201.

Pages 164-65 A follower of Christ is different: *Mere Christianity,* p. 164.

Page 165   "The Christian is called": "Membership," *Fern-seed,* p. 15.

Page 165   "God communicates His presence": *Reflections on the Psalms,* p. 93.

Page 165   " 'The fair beauty of the Lord' is revealed": Ibid.

Page 165   "I must keep alive in myself": *Mere Christianity,* p. 120.

Page 165   "Every Christian is to become": Ibid., p. 153.

Page 165   "Putting on Christ": Ibid., p. 166.

Page 165   "All day long": *Problem of Pain,* p. 63.

Page 167   "Sleep, sweat, footsore weariness": *Letters to Malcolm,* pp. 70-71.
Page 168   "The whole purpose for which we exist": *Mere Christianity,* p. 141.
Page 168   *Mere Christianity,* bk. 2, chap. 4: "The Perfect Penitent."
Page 168   We start by expanding the circle: See *Mere Christianity,* p. 98.

BIBLIOGRAPHY

Books by C. S. Lewis

The Abolition of Man. 1943. Reprint, New York: Macmillan, 1973.

All My Road Before Me: The Diary of C. S. Lewis, 1922-1927. Edited by Walter Hooper. San Diego: Harcourt Brace Jovanovich, 1991.

The Allegory of Love. 1936. Reprint, London: Oxford University Press, 1973.

Christian Reflections. Edited by Walter Hooper. Grand Rapids: Eerdmans, 1973.

The Collected Letters of C. S. Lewis, Volume 1: *Family Letters 1905-1931.* Edited by Walter Hooper. London: HarperCollins, 2000.

The Collected Letters of C. S. Lewis, Volume 2: *Books, Broadcasts, and the War, 1931-1949.* Edited by Walter Hooper. London: HarperCollins, 2004.

The Discarded Image. 1964. Reprint, Cambridge: Cambridge University Press, 1971.

Dymer. London: J. M. Dent, 1926. Reprint, New York: Macmillan, 1950.

English Literature in the Sixteenth Century, Excluding Drama. Oxford: Clarendon Press, 1954.

An Experiment in Criticism. Cambridge: Cambridge University Press, 1961.

Fern-seed and Elephants and Other Essays on Christianity. Edited by Walter Hooper. New York: Collins, 1977.

The Four Loves. New York: Harcourt Brace Jovanovich, 1960.

George MacDonald: An Anthology. Edited by C. S. Lewis. Garden City, N.Y.: Doubleday, 1962.

God in the Dock: Essays on Theology and Ethics. Edited by Walter Hooper. Grand Rapids: Eerdmans, 1970.

The Great Divorce. 1946. Reprint, New York: Fontana, 1972.

A Grief Observed. London: Faber & Faber, 1961.

The Horse and His Boy. 1954. Reprint, New York: Collier, 1970.

The Last Battle. 1956. Reprint, New York: Collier, 1970.

Letters: C. S. Lewis/Don Giovanni Calabria. Translated and edited by Martin Moynihan. Ann Arbor, Mich.: Servant Books, 1989.

Letters of C. S. Lewis. Edited by W. H. Lewis. London: HarperCollins, 1966. Revised by Walter Hooper, 1988.

Letters to an American Lady. Edited by Clyde S. Kilby. Grand Rapids: Eerdmans, 1967.

Letters to Children. Edited by Lyle W. Dorsett and Marjorie Lamp Mead. New York: Macmillan, 1985.

Letters to Malcolm: Chiefly on Prayer. New York: Harcourt Brace Jovanovich, 1964.

The Lion, the Witch and the Wardrobe. 1950. Reprint, New York: Collier, 1970.

The Magician's Nephew. 1955. Reprint, New York: Collier, 1970.

Mere Christianity. 1952. Reprint, New York: Macmillan, 1969.

Miracles: A Preliminary Study. 1947. Reprint, New York: Macmillan, 1968.

Narrative Poems. Edited by Walter Hooper. London: Geoffrey Bles, 1969.

Of Other Worlds: Essays and Stories. Edited by Walter Hooper. New York: Harcourt Brace Jovanovich, 1975.

On Stories and Other Essays on Literature. New York: Harcourt Brace Jovanovich, 1982.

Out of the Silent Planet. 1938. Reprint, New York: Macmillan, 1968.

Perelandra. 1943. Reprint, New York: Macmillan, 1968.

The Personal Heresy: A Controversy. 1939. Reprint, London: Oxford University Press, 1965.

The Pilgrim's Regress. 1933. Reprint, New York: Harcourt Brace Jovanovich, 1960.

Poems. Edited by Walter Hooper. New York: Harcourt Brace Jovanovich, 1964.

A Preface to Paradise Lost. 1942. Reprint, London: Oxford University Press, 1970.

Present Concerns. Edited by Walter Hooper. San Diego: Harcourt Brace Jovanovich, 1987.

Prince Caspian. 1951. Reprint, New York: Collier, 1970.

The Problem of Pain. 1940. Reprint, London: Collins, 1972.

Reflections on the Psalms. 1958. Reprint, New York: Harcourt Brace Jovanovich, 1982.

Rehabilitations and Other Essays. London: Oxford University Press, 1939.

The Screwtape Letters. 1942. Reprint, New York: Macmillan, 1960.

Screwtape Proposes a Toast and Other Pieces. London: Collins, 1970.

Selected Literary Essays. Edited by Walter Hooper. Cambridge: Cambridge University Press, 1966.

The Silver Chair. 1953. Reprint, New York: Collier, 1970.

Spenser's Images of Life. Edited by Alistair Fowler. Cambridge: Cambridge University Press, 1967.

Spirits in Bondage: A Cycle of Lyrics. 1919. Reprint, New York: Harcourt Brace Jovanovich, 1984.

Studies in Medieval and Renaissance Literature. Edited by Walter Hooper. Cambridge: Cambridge University Press, 1969.

Studies in Words. Cambridge: Cambridge University Press, 1960.

Surprised by Joy: The Shape of My Early Life. New York: Harcourt Brace Jovanovich, 1955.

That Hideous Strength: A Modern Fairy-Tale for Grown-Ups. 1945. Reprint, New York: Macmillan, 1968.

They Stand Together: The Letters of C. S. Lewis to Arthur Greeves (1914-1963). Edited by Walter Hooper. New York: Macmillan, 1979.

Till We Have Faces. 1956. Reprint, Grand Rapids: Eerdmans, 1966.

The Voyage of the "Dawn Treader." 1952. Reprint, New York: Collier, 1970.

The Weight of Glory and Other Addresses. 1949. Reprint, Grand Rapids: Eerdmans, 1965.

The World's Last Night and Other Essays. New York: Harcourt Brace Jovanovich, 1960.

Resources on C. S. Lewis

Como, James T., ed. *"C. S. Lewis at the Breakfast Table" and Other Reminiscences.* New York: Macmillan, 1979.

Flieger, Verlyn. "The Sound of Silence: Language and Experience in *Out of the Silent Planet.*" In *Word and Story in C. S. Lewis.* Edited by Peter J. Schakel and Charles A. Huttar. Columbia: University of Missouri Press, 1991.

Glover, Donald E. *C. S. Lewis and the Art of Enchantment.* Athens: Ohio University Press, 1981.

Green, Roger Lancelyn and Walter Hooper. *C. S. Lewis: A Biography.* Revised edition. San Diego: Harvest Books, 1994.

Harmon, Kendall. "Nothingness and Human Destiny: Hell in the Thought of C. S. Lewis." In *The Pilgrim's Guide: C. S. Lewis and the Art of Witness*. Edited by David Mills. Grand Rapids: Eerdmans, 1998.

Hooper, Walter. *C. S. Lewis: A Companion and Guide*. San Francisco: HarperSanFrancisco, 1996.

———— "C. S. Lewis: The Man and His Thought." In *Essays on C. S. Lewis and George MacDonald*. Edited by Cynthia Marshall. Lewiston, N.Y.: Edwin Mellen, 1991.

Lindskoog, Kathryn. "Links in a Golden Chain: C. S. Lewis, George MacDonald, and Sadhu Sundar Singh." *The Lewis Legacy* 69 (1996).

Moynihan, Martin. "I Sleep but My Heart Watcheth." In *We Remember C. S. Lewis: Essays and Memoirs*. Edited by David Graham. Nashville: Broadman & Holman, 2001.

Root, Jerry. "Tools Inadequate and Incomplete: C. S. Lewis and the Great Religions." In *The Pilgrim's Guide: C. S. Lewis and the Art of Witness*. Edited by David Mills. Grand Rapids: Eerdmans, 1998.

Sayer, George. *Jack: C. S. Lewis and His Times*. San Francisco: Harper & Row, 1988.

Taliaferro, Charles. "A Narnian Theory of Atonement." *Scottish Journal of Theology* 41 (1988): 75-92.

Walsh, Chad. *The Literary Legacy of C. S. Lewis*. New York: Harcourt Brace Jovanovich, 1979.

Ware, Kallistos. "God of the Fathers: C. S. Lewis and Eastern Christianity." In *The Pilgrim's Guide: C. S. Lewis and the Art of Witness*. Edited by David Mills. Grand Rapids: Eerdmans, 1998.

Resources on Mystics and Mysticism

Armstrong, Karen. *Visions of God: Four Medieval Mystics and Their Writings*. New York: Bantam, 1994.

Augustine. *The City of God*. Edited by Vernon J. Bourke. Garden City, N.Y.: Image, 1958.

————. *Confessions*. Translated by Albert C. Outler. Philadelphia: Westminster Press, 1915.

————. *Confessions*. Translated by Henry Chadwick. Oxford: Oxford University Press, 1992.

Baker, Denise Nowakowski. *Julian of Norwich's Showings: From Vision to Book.* Princeton, N.J.: Princeton University Press, 1994.

Balfour, Arthur James. *Theism and Humanism.* London: Hodder & Stoughton, 1915.

Baumgardt, David. *The Great Western Mystics: Their Lasting Significance.* New York: Columbia University Press, 1961.

Beer, Francis. *Women and Mystical Experience in the Middle Ages.* Woodbridge, England: Boydell & Brewer, 1993.

Bevan, Edwyn. *Symbolism and Belief.* London: Allen & Unwin, 1938.

Boehme, Jacob. *The Signature of All Things and Other Writings.* London: James Clark, 1969.

Bruce, F. F. "Was Paul a Mystic?" *The Reformed Theological Review* 34 (1975).

Butler, Cuthbert. *Western Mysticism.* New York: Dutton, 1923.

Capps, Walter Holden and Wendy M. Wright, eds. *Silent Fire: An Invitation to Western Mysticism.* San Francisco: Harper & Row, 1968.

Catherine of Siena. *The Dialogue.* Translated by Suzanne Noffke. New York: Paulist Press, 1980.

Chesterton, G. K. *All Things Considered.* New York: Sheed & Ward, 1956.

————. *The Everlasting Man.* New York: Dodd, Mead, 1925. Reprint, San Francisco: Ignatius, 1993.

————. *Varied Types.* New York: Dodd, Mead, 1908.

————. *William Blake.* London: Duckworth, 1910.

Christopher, J. R. *Evelyn Underhill.* Grand Rapids: Eerdmans, 1975.

Comer, Kim, ed. *Wisdom of the Sadhu: Teachings of Sundar Singh.* Farmington, Penn.: Plough, 2000.

Cook, Edward. *The Life of Florence Nightingale.* New York: Macmillan, 1942.

Corduan, Winfried. *Mysticism: An Evangelical Option?* Grand Rapids: Zondervan, 1991.

Earle, William. "Phenomenology of Mysticism." In *Experience of the Sacred: Readings in the Phenomenology of Religion.* Edited by Summer R. Twiss and Walter H. Conser Jr. Providence, R.I.: Brown University Press, 1992.

Egan, Harvey D. *An Anthology of Christian Mysticism.* 2nd ed. Collegeville, Minn.: Liturgical Press, 1996.

————. *Christian Mysticism: The Future of a Tradition.* Collegeville, Minn.: Liturgical Press, 1990.

Flanagan, Sabina. *Hildegard of Bingen, 1098-1179: A Visionary Life.* London: Routledge, 1989.

Forman, Robert K. C. *Mysticism, Mind, Consciousness.* Albany: State University of New York Press, 1999.

Fraser, Stephen. "Newly Released Letters Tell of Jesus Calling Mother Teresa 'My Little Wife.' " *Scotland on Sunday,* December 8, 2002. Quoting from a biography by Saverio Gaeta, *Mother Teresa's Secret* <http://news.scotsman.com/international.cfm?id=1367572002>.

Freemantle, Anne, ed. *The Protestant Mystics.* Boston: Little, Brown, 1964.

Gem, Harvey S. *The Mysticism of William Law.* New York: E. S. Gorham, 1914.

Gimello, Robert. "Mysticism and Meditation." In *Mysticism and Philosophical Analysis.* Edited by Steven Katz. New York: Oxford University Press, 1978.

Graef, Hilda. *The Story of Mysticism.* Garden City, N.Y.: Doubleday, 1965.

Green, Julien. *God's Fool: The Life and Times of Francis of Assisi.* Translated by Peter Heinegg. San Francisco: Harper & Row, 1985.

Guiley, Rosemary Ellen, ed. *Harper's Encyclopedia of Mystical and Paranormal Experience.* New York: HarperCollins, 1991.

Hadfield, Alice Mary. *Charles Williams: An Exploration of His Life and Work.* New York: Oxford University Press, 1983.

Happold, F. C. *Mysticism: A Study and Anthology.* London: Penguin, 1963.

Harkness, Georgia. *Mysticism: Its Meaning and Message.* Nashville: Abingdon, 1973.

Heath-Stubbs, John. *Charles Williams.* London: Longmans, Green, 1955.

Hein, Rolland. *The Harmony Within: The Spiritual Vision of George MacDonald.* Grand Rapids: Christian University Press, 1983.

Hick, John. "Mystical Spirit as Cognition." In *Understanding Mysticism.* Edited by Richard P. Woods. Garden City, N.Y.: Image Books, 1980.

Hilton, Walter. *The Scale of Perfection.* Translated by John P. H. Clark and Rosemary Dorward. New York: Paulist Press, 1991.

Hoagland, Victor C. P. *The Book of Saints.* New York: Regina, 1986.

Horgan, John. *Rational Mysticism: Dispatches from the Border Between Science and Spirituality.* Boston: Houghton Mifflin, 2003.

Hügel, Baron Friedrich von. *Eternal Life: A Study of Its Applications and Implications.* Edinburgh: T & T Clark, 1913.

Huxley, Aldous. *The Doors of Perception.* New York: Harper & Row, 1954. Reprint 1990.

————. *The Perennial Philosophy.* New York: Harper & Row, 1945.

Inge, William R. *Christian Mysticism.* New York: Charles Scribner's, 1902.

James, Bruno S. *Saint Bernard of Clairvaux: An Essay in Biography.* London: Hodder and Stoughton, 1957.

James, William. *The Varieties of Religious Experience.* London: Longmans, Green, 1902.

Jones, Rufus M. *The Flowering of Mysticism: The Friends of God in the Fourteenth Century.* New York: Macmillan, 1939.

Joy, James Richard. *John Wesley's Awakening.* New York: Methodist Books, 1937.

Julian of Norwich. *Showings.* Translated by Edmund Colledge and James Walsh. New York: Paulist Press, 1978.

Kavanaugh, Kieran. *John of the Cross: Doctor of Light and Love.* New York: Crossroad, 1999.

King, Ursula. *The Christian Mystics: Their Lives and Legacies Throughout the Ages.* Mahwah, N.J.: Hidden Spring, 2001.

Law, William. *Liberal and Mystical Writings of William Law.* New York: Longmans, Green, 1908.

Loxton, Howard. *The Encyclopedia of Saints.* Stamford, Conn.: Longmeadow, 1996.

McCann, Justin, ed. *The Cloud of Unknowing.* London: Burns Oates, 1960.

McGinn, Bernard. *The Presence of God: A History of Western Christian Mysticism.* 5 vols. New York: Crossroad, 1998. (The five volumes are *The Foundations of Mysticism: Origins to the Fifth Century* [1991]; *The Growth of Mysticism: From Gregory the Great to the Twelfth Century* [1994]; *The Flowering of Mysticism: Men and Women in the New Mysticism, 1200-1350* [1998]; *Continuity and Change in Western Mysticism* [forthcoming]; *The Crisis in Western Mysticism* [forthcoming].)

Miller, Gordon L. *The Way of the English Mystics.* Ridgefield, Conn.: Morehouse, 1996.

O'Connell, Marvin R. *Blaise Pascal: Reasons of the Heart.* Grand Rapids: Eerdmans, 1997.

Otto, Rudolf. *The Idea of the Holy.* Translated by John W. Harvey. London: Oxford University Press, 1923.

————. *Mysticism East and West: A Comparative Analysis of the Nature of Mysticism.* Translated by Bertha L. Bracey and Richenda C. Payne. New York: Macmillan, 1932.

Parker, Arthur. *Sadhu Sundar Singh: Called of God.* London: Revell, 1920.

Schweitzer, Albert. *The Mysticism of Paul the Apostle.* Translated by William Montgomery. New York: Macmillan, 1955.

Shideler, Mary McDermott. *Charles Williams.* Grand Rapids: Eerdmans, 1966.

Söderblom, Nathan. *The Living God.* Oxford: Oxford University Press, 1933.

St. John of the Cross. *The Collected Works of St. John of the Cross.* Translated by Kieran Kavanaugh and Otilio Rodriguez. Washington, D.C.: Institute of Carmelite Studies, 1973.

Stace, W. T. *Mysticism and Philosophy.* New York: Macmillan, 1960.

Steel, Francesca Maria. *The Life and Visions of St. Hildegard.* London: Herder, 1915.

Streeter, Burnett Hillman and Aiyadurai Jesudasen Appasamy. *The Message of Sadhu Sundar Singh: A Study in Mysticism and Practical Religion.* New York: Macmillan, 1922.

Teresa of Ávila. *The Interior Castle.* Translated by E. Allison Peers. Garden City, N.Y.: Doubleday, 1989.

———. *The Life of Saint Teresa of Avila by Herself.* Translated by J. M. Cohen. London: Penguin, 1957.

Thurston, Herbert. *The Physical Phenomena of Mysticism.* Chicago: Henry Regnery, 1952.

Underhill, Evelyn. *The Letters of Evelyn Underhill.* Edited by Charles Williams. London: Longmans, Green, 1943.

———. *Mysticism.* London: Methuen, 1911.

———. *The Mystics of the Church.* New York: Schocken, 1964.

Weeks, Andrew. *German Mysticism from Hildegard of Bingen to Ludwig Wittgenstein.* New York: State University of New York Press, 1983.

Williams, Charles. *The Descent of the Dove: A Short History of the Holy Spirit in the Church.* Grand Rapids: Eerdmans, 1939.

———. *He Came Down from Heaven.* London: William Heinemann, 1938.

Winkworth, Susanna, trans. *Theologia Germanica.* Philadelphia: George W. McCalla, 1887.

Woods, Richard, ed. *Understanding Mysticism.* Garden City, N.Y.: Doubleday, 1980.

Wright, Wendy M., ed. *Francis de Sales: "Introduction to the Devout Life" and "Treatise on the Love of God."* New York: Crossroad, 1997.

Zaehner, R. C. *Mysticism: Sacred and Profane.* Oxford: Oxford University Press, 1957.

Subject Index

Scripture Index